How We Seek God Together

EXPLORING WORSHIP STYLE

Linda J. Clark

Joanne Swenson

Mark Stamm

Foreword by Don E. Saliers

The Alban Institute

Copyright © 2001 by the Alban Institute. All rights reserved.

This material may not be photocopied or reproduced in any way without written permission.

Library of Congress Card Number 00-111202

ISBN 1-56699-242-7

CONTENTS

101063

There can be little doubt that Christian congregations in North America are undergoing a period of change and turmoil about the style and substance of public worship. A period of intense concentration on liturgical reforms across a wide ecumenical spectrum followed the Second Vatican Council in the last decades of the twentieth century. Most mainline denominations undertook to revise their principal rites, texts, and worship books.

Our current situation goes well beyond matters of textual revisions and new hymnals, however. We now face difficult issues produced by the presence of multiple cultures within denominations and local churches, and the impact of larger forces that forge the tastes, expectations, and desires people bring to worship. Conflicts between those who favor so-called traditional and contemporary forms of worship are but a symptom of the turmoil. As over-simplified as these terms are, they point to questions about the complex character of Christian congregations at worship.

To understand how and why we worship as we do, we need more than worship books or the bulletins can possibly reveal. Reflection on the places, practices, and emerging life patterns that inform worship is required. Christian worship has always been culturally embodied and embedded. Only recently have we become aware of how this truth bears upon the theology and faith shaped and expressed in the local assembly at worship. This connection between culture and theology is perhaps most obvious when we ask questions such as, "Whose music?" "Which instruments?" Congregations are often in conflict over questions of appropriateness and faithfulness. None of these questions will produce fruitful results unless leaders of congregations are prepared to study the people who worship—their cultural habitations and expectations.

It turns out, as the authors of *How We Seek God Together* are convinced, that such a study is about both real life and living theology. This book helps us to explore several crucial aspects of the worshiping assembly. It makes a strong case for examining the inner relationship between the style or styles of worship and the piety of congregational life. By studying in detail three distinctively different Methodist congregations in Massachusetts, the collaborative research team both models and invites a significant method for self-study. The authors present and provoke pastoral, theological, and liturgical discussion. Those concerned with gaining insight into the ethos of actual worship will find here a valuable set of resources. By focusing on the relationship between style and piety, the authors offer a significant way to analyze and understand deeper background issues with which Christian churches are currently dealing.

We learn from Linda Clark and her colleagues, for example, that because the worship life of any given congregation is woven together in complex ways with the unspoken patterns of members' lives, the study of worship requires attention to the distinctive local cultures of the congregation.

We also are shown how people's participation in worship is difficult to understand unless we pay attention to the interiorization of faith that exists in a given congregation. At the heart of this book is a conviction that the style of worship discloses key aspects of a congregation's theological center of gravity—its substantive piety. The style of worship is not simply an external illustration of the congregation's ideas and images of God. Rather, style *shapes* the ideas and images of the divine, just as such ideas and images shape the sense of style in a given worshiping assembly.

These observations might remind some of us of Marshall McLuhan's famous observation that the medium is the message. Thus style is not a surface matter, and piety is more than merely the felt experience of faith. Piety includes both reflective and prereflective dimensions of theology, as actual lived faith—the collective spirituality of the faith community and its various constituencies.

We are taken inside the life of these three congregations by the portraits. No claim to exhaustive analysis is made. Instead, these portraits become vivid touchstones for the range of factors emerging in any such study of a local congregation. In the pages that follow, we find not so much a definitive study as a set of resources for further research. The portraits of these congregations should serve as a catalyst to a fresh form of congregational analysis focusing on the centrality of the worship life. In these pages we are compelled to consider through multiple perspectives the way a style of worship, especially in its musical and aesthetic aspects, both shapes and expresses the primary theology of the community.

The *Constitution on the Sacred Liturgy* of Vatican II called Christian liturgy the "source and summit" of the Christian life. Though the research does not tell the whole story of each of the case study congregations, these narrative accounts reveal powerful insights into the centrality of worship in the life of local churches. With the videotape juxtaposed to the data, you will find yourself saying, "I know these people," because, despite the distinctiveness of each, the human factors that surface suggest cross-cultural analogies as well.

Above all we can learn this: the words we use in the worship of God depend radically on what is not verbal for their meaning. The nonverbal dimensions (sound, sight, gesture, movement, and symbols), beyond the cognitive and explicitly conscious features of what we do, are essential to understanding the inner relationships between style and piety. What emerges here is an effective and flexible method for the study of any congregation's worship life. This book will help many pastors and worship leaders, along with congregations who undertake self-study, to approach a goal we so much desire. How can we bring Christian worship to real life and our real lives to God in faithful worship? As the great liturgical scholar Dom Gregory Dix once observed, the study of worship is always the study of the real lives of men and women.

DON E. SALIERS

This book and its accompanying videotape are a report of the findings of the Worship, Music, and Religious Identity Research Project, undertaken in the early 1990s by the authors and others at Boston University School of Theology, and funded by the Lilly Endowment, Inc., of Indianapolis. From the beginning it has been a collaboration among the research team, the filmmaker, numerous other advisors, and the people in the three congregations who graciously invited us into their churches and their lives. The writing of the book has been the responsibility of Linda J. Clark, principal investigator for the research project, who wrote the introduction and chapters 1, 4, and 5. Joanne Swenson wrote chapter 2 and Mark Stamm chapter 3. The reader will notice that the three central chapters dealing with the congregations differ in their approach and their style—an important concept in our mutual endeavor. We brought a variety of interests and expertise to the research and the writing, which is borne out in these chapters. We see this diversity as one of the great strengths of the book and of our collaboration throughout the research.

At this point it is fitting to mention with affection and gratitude the fourth member of our research team, Greg Allen, a biblical scholar who contributed his time, energy, and commitment to our work during the research phase. Indeed, most of the content was generated in the lively exchange of ideas during the course of the research project, the ensuing analysis, and the three conferences we held in Boston to test out our growing understanding of the interrelationship of style and piety. Thus what you find here is based on the work of hundreds of people: church leaders, musicians, pastors; and scholars of worship, music, and congregational studies.

I would like to single out two other people for special mention. The first is James Ault, film director, who spent much time in the congregations and with the research team, questioning us about the nature of the research and its relationship to the worship life of these congregations. Then, working with a film crew, he managed to capture the distinctiveness of these congregations at worship. It was a monumentally difficult task, undertaken with consummate skill and imagination. His success is central to the success of the research that is reported in this book. Thank you, Jim.

The other person is Tim Hughes, our administrative associate. Even before submitting the initial grant proposal to the Lilly Endowment, I checked to make sure that Tim was available for the task. Research as complex as this required an administrative genius, and he had proved to be such a one in the past. His success undergirds the success of the research as well. Thank you, Tim.

I am also indebted to the people at the Lilly Endowment, Inc., of Indianapolis, and to James P. Wind, president of the Alban Institute, for their support of the research and their encouragement of my work. None of this would have taken place without their generous support.

And last, but certainly not least, I would like to thank the people in the three congregations who graciously agreed to take part in the study. Our presence among you caused you difficulties at times. We appreciate the sacrifices you made, the confusion and consternation you endured on our behalf. You taught us all much about the nature of faith and inspired us in our work among you. Your success is a key to the success of this educational endeavor.

THANK YOU:

Carter Memorial United Methodist Church
of Needham, Massachusetts.

Columbus Avenue African Methodist Episcopal Zion Church
of Boston, Massachusetts.

Community United Methodist Church
of Byfield, Massachusetts.

LINDA J. CLARK

The Worship, Music, and Religious Identity Research Project

S everal years ago, Anne Ford, a graduate of the master of sacred music program at Boston University School of Theology, took a job in a Congregational church in an affluent suburb not far from a major highway leading into Boston. She was a talented musician and a superb choral conductor. She was brought to the church during an interim period. The senior minister had left, and the associate minister, a friend of Anne's, had been filling in until a new minister could be called. The search for a minister was protracted and contentious. In the meantime, Anne settled in, established a good working relationship with the existing staff and lay leadership, and began to build a strong music program.

The search committee finally found a candidate about whom everyone was enthusiastic. He was from another region of the country and seemed to be a welcome change for this reserved New England community. In the course of the final interview, he expressed a desire that his wife, who wrote and sang hymns in a popular folk style, work with Anne in the music program. This request threw the interview process off, because people did not want the minister's wife to derail what Anne had begun. Anne's style was eclectic, but based firmly in the classical tradition. So the search committee thanked the minister for his suggestions but made it clear that, although they welcomed the efforts of his wife, Anne was clearly in charge of the music program. Everyone agreed, and he was called to the church.

It did not take long for things to fall apart. The senior minister would occasionally insist that his wife's hymns be sung in worship, no matter what the music director's plans. Some people loved these songs, and others hated them. Anne was in the latter camp, but she dutifully worked with the minister's wife nonetheless. Other problems surfaced among the staff and in the congregation—problems that would have split any group regardless of the minister's wife and her hymns. However, the music became the battleground on which the issues were fought out. In the end, the associate pastor and Anne resigned, and the senior minister and his family left the congregation.

What went on in that church? How could something so seemingly innocuous as the style of a hymn cause such a furor? This book—an in-depth discussion of worship styles and their religious import—will give insight into the depth and causes of such conflicts. It is based on a series of studies of worship practices in local congregations. Initially, the research team fanned out among various Methodist churches in the Boston area, looking for likely congregations. We wanted to find three churches whose styles of worship were very different from one another. To qualify, a church had to exemplify its particular style clearly; that is, it had to do what it did on Sunday very well. We wanted to remain within the confines of one denomination or tradition and yet find congregations whose styles of worship would be sharply contrasting. What we hoped to find were three churches with similar worship patterns executed in different ways. We ended up with two United Methodist churches, one in a rural town and the other in a suburb of Boston, and one African Methodist Episcopal Zion church in Boston itself. Each vividly exemplified a particular style of worship.

It is difficult to study worship. In worshiping, we create and work with symbols and forms, many of them centuries old. In a lifetime, we do not exhaust their meaning. But, more important, as we do this work of worship, God is there with us, working in ways that frequently exceed human knowing. How can any group of people presume to scrutinize such a powerful and often mysterious activity under the lens of a microscope? The answer: with great humility.

This book tries to answer the question: "What is the religious import of a congregation's style of worship?" Every congregation has a certain "feel" or "tone." It does things in a certain way. Some churches are formal, some informal; some openly friendly, others more reserved and focused inward. What can one learn about the many ways that people of faith worship God by studying the style of their gatherings? That may at first seem a silly question—even trivial. Why study the way things are done? Isn't the style just packaging? Why not go right to the "meat"—the content? However, style is a crucial subject for study, as we learned. Many congregations today are locked in conflict about worship style—the style of the music and the way the service is conducted on Sunday morning. That widespread conflict is one of the reasons we began looking into style. We found that style conflict was just the tip of a massive iceberg. The deeper we went, the more style became a profound subject. Later we will define and illustrate more fully what we mean by the term *style*. Style is an attribute of a congregation, displaying its uniqueness. It grows out of the parish's history, its culture, its tradition. Style is a signature of a church's faith life.

Congregational Research at Boston University

This research project grew out of previous work that we at Boston University had done examining music programs in 24 Episcopal and United Methodist churches in New England (1987–1990; published by the Alban Institute in 1995 as *Music in Churches*.). In that project, we sent researchers into churches to find out how ordinary people—musicians, congregants, pastors, lay leaders—made connections between music and the life of faith. We handed out questionnaires to people at worship in all 24 churches; we then chose eight churches that represented differing patterns and styles of worship as sites for case studies. In those, we conducted interviews and visited staff meetings, potluck suppers, choir rehearsals, and so forth. Two researchers arrived unannounced on a Sunday to observe each church at worship.

At the outset of that study we had naïvely hoped to find churches that were free of conflict. We knew that conducting a study in a church is a major intervention in its ongoing life, and we did not want to aggravate an already difficult situation. However, we found conflict of varying kinds and degrees of intensity wherever we went. Much of it centered on the music programs. In some instances, music was the battleground for other issues—power, conflicts in styles of leadership—but some of the conflict dealt specifically with the style of music employed in worship. These churches were coping with their disagreements in various ways. In some communities, a consensus had been established; in some, worship of differing styles was scheduled at separate hours on Sunday; in others, the one Sunday service included many styles of music. In still others, the debate raged on among staff and lay leaders, with no compromise in sight.

It is this increased congregational interest in patterns of worship and the conflicts and discussion generated by that interest that led to the study of "Worship, Music, and Religious Identity (1992–1996)." A research team composed of Linda J. Clark, a church musician and historical musicologist; Mark Stamm, a Methodist liturgical scholar; Joanne Swenson, a theologian; and Greg Allen, a biblical scholar; studied the styles of music and worship in three Methodist congregations a short car or trolley ride from Boston University.

Clark has a doctorate of music from Union Theological Seminary in New York. She is director of the master of sacred music program at the Boston University School of Theology, where she has been a faculty member since 1980, and is now James R. Houghton scholar of sacred music. She lives in Boston with her husband, an Episcopal priest, and attends her local Episcopal parish.

Stamm, who has a doctorate of theology in liturgical studies from Boston University School of Theology, is an ordained United Methodist pastor. He teaches at Perkins School of Theology at Southern Methodist University in Dallas, and lives in Dallas with his wife and two sons. Stamm is a member of the Order of St. Luke, a Methodist organization advocating worship renewal.

Swenson, who earned a Ph.D. in theology from Harvard University, is ordained as a United Church of Christ pastor. She lives with her husband and two children in Portland, Oregon. There she attends a Presbyterian church with a charismatic worship style.

The Research Methodology

A member of the research team was assigned to each of the three congregations. We began attending worship in each church on Palm Sunday one spring and stopped the next spring after Easter. Thus we could compare our reactions to Holy Week at the beginning and end of the immersion in the field site. During that time we took field notes, ran a series of one-on-one interviews, sent out a questionnaire to those on the church rolls, and videotaped the congregation at worship. James Ault, a filmmaker, directed the shoot and edited the tapes, creating one for each congregation. Each of these tapes included about 30 minutes of the congregation at worship, and 12 minutes of intercuts, showing in quick succession the three congregations engaged in ordinary acts of worship. Thus the ending of each film showed clips of the three processions, the three sermons, the choirs, the singing, the praying, and so forth.

We went back to the three congregations, showed the videotapes, and conducted focus group interviews. Although we were particularly interested in the music, it was one of many ingredients of Sunday morning that interested us. We also studied the style of the preaching, the praying, the way parishioners gathered, what they did with the children, the amount and type of ritual movement, and so forth. In our interviews in each congregation, we recorded the congregants' own words as they described worship. It is their interpretation of worship—the insider's view—that we captured in the interviews. After an initial analysis of the data, we went back to the three congregations for their feedback. This stage of the project resulted in many discussions in which our observations of a congregation at worship were tested and reshaped.

What you will find in this resource is a series of snapshots of people in congregations. They are impressionistic rather than comprehensive. It is not our intent to provide an exhaustive picture of worship and music in these churches. No one person or group—whether insider or outsider—could ever adequately sum up the worship life of a community in all its depth and mystery. We went into these communities to investigate the relationship between style and faith, or piety. While there we sought to record the congregants' own way of talking about their worship—what they found meaningful, how they related it to their own lives within the walls of the church as well as in the institutions where they worked, played, raised their children, and coped with the vagaries of life. In each videotape we juxtaposed the church's worship style beside the others to help parishioners see that what they took for granted as normal worship behavior might have certain qualities that others' worship did not. We used a comparative method to lead them to see their world as unique and to become aware of it in a different way. In the interviews comparisons among the three churches were made by the congregants. These often provided us with valuable information about their piety. When someone remarked, "Our church is more spiritual," we asked why. However, we were not there to make these comparisons ourselves. To the extent that we could, we bracketed our own biases, our own backgrounds, our own judgments.

We make no claims of complete objectivity, nor do we insist that what we have here is the "honest truth" about the worship in three churches. Like all researchers, we brought an interpretive perspective to our work. In focusing on certain aspects of church life and excluding others, we built in certain limitations. This inherent bias extends to the analysis as well.

Certain characteristics popped out at us, while others got less attention. Within these pages, the researchers occasionally offer their own points of view. Those sections are labeled "Observer's Comments," as they were in our field notes. We describe our own cultural perspective before making these comments.

The data—interviews, field notes, videotapes, questionnaire results, historical notes—provide the basis for the analysis. We listened to the data "speak," and then drew certain conclusions from it. The book is not just a report of what we found. We brought concepts to the task and developed concepts from the data. We stepped back from the trees to describe the forest. We developed conclusions from this forest. Because of the importance of worship to the religious lives of the people in these congregations, we approached our analytical tasks in humility.[1]

The Findings

We have come to four conclusions about the churches in the project:

1. On Sunday morning, each of these communities is involved in the same religious process in differing guises—that is, each is engaged in a search for conversion.

2. The images of God and of the faithful that are embedded in their styles of worship differ, and sometimes profoundly.

3. In the interviews, people speak of worship as bearing great transcendent moments—times of great depth and force, when the songs, prayers, and rites are experienced as "the Habitation of the Most High."

4. Yet people also speak of worship in their church as a barrier to God: the same style that has the possibility of transcendence also at times masks or denies the fullness of God.

In a kind of shorthand, we termed instances of conclusions 3 and 4 as "breakout" and "breakdown." It is important to underscore the fact that a particular style can be an instance of both. Each congregational style had its own special temptation. Here we are not simply speaking about the sort of breakdown that we see occasionally in weekly Sunday worship—someone tripping on the way down the aisle during the procession, the dropped choir music, the pastor getting the hiccups in the middle of communion. It is a more systemic failure having to do with human nature and its limitations. Let us briefly illustrate what we mean by these two terms.

Perhaps the most dramatic *breakout* point of worship in the three services we videotaped was the response to the pastor's altar call at Columbus Avenue AME Zion Church. In later interviews, we asked people of that congregation to describe what this moment meant to them. Said one parishioner:

> In everything we do, there are two ultimate ends. One is for our own souls to be saved and to keep in communication and contact with the Savior, and [the second is] to save others and to evangelize. To bring others into the fold of safety—into the fold of Christ—so that becomes a very vital part of the sermon, because the Word of God is not supposed to go out and come back void. And void means no one has heard it, no one has joined, no one has come with us. So when a person joins, the Word of God has gone out, been heard—and his coming [into the fold] fulfills it.

Another remarked:

> The term that we use is "an invitation to Christian discipleship," so when they are walking into the fold, [the class leaders surround one who comes] and say, "OK, you've come into the fold, O lost sheep!" and we embrace him. That person is saying, "I've been out there and now I'm coming in!"

The sermon is also a part of this movement to the altar:

> I also believe it comes through the message when the reverend is preaching. I believe the message you receive, you can feel it; you can really feel it in your chest. And they only don't hear it through the minister; they also hear it through God, and it's time—God is saying that it's time now for you to come home. And sometimes a person has no control, because you don't know what you're going to do. You just get up and you just go.

At the end of worship that Sunday with the film crew present, in the midst of the singing and praying, a young man answered the pastor's call to the altar. The power of that act filled the room. Later interviewees described it as someone answering the voice of God, calling the sinner home: "It's time now for you to come home!"

In another interview in the same congregation, one hears of worship *breakdown*. In one of the focus groups, people disagreed about whether being active and upbeat in worship—standing up, clapping hands, giving the preacher and the singers an "Amen!" or "That's right!"—was essential to worship. One person—"A" below—was adamant about the importance of being "in the Spirit" within a group of people also "in the Spirit." Another—"B" below—was adamant about allowing for a diversity of expression, especially the option to sit quietly.

A: I can remember when our church did not have all of the fire that it has now. Back then it was very quiet, and it was very black and very cold, and I used to sit there and wonder, "What are we going to do to liven up this place, because the church is going to die if something doesn't change." And they got some of these fellows from over at the Holy Rollers section of the table [laughter], and they fired it up, but we have to thank them.

B: The older people that were here that believed in that type of worship—that was the people of the time. The time changed. Those people believed that they could feel just as good as anybody else and have just as much spirit and praising God by just sitting there, keeping quiet. And there are those who do not believe that they can do that. They believe that you can't have the Spirit unless you are emotional, but I do believe that those old people that were there had just as much religion as anybody else.

A: But I can't disagree . . . but if you've got the Spirit, something'll come out of you. You just can't sit there and be—

B: That's your way of thinking.

The people involved in this exchange were arguing about the power of a style of worship to carry a transcendent moment. For "A," the older patterns of worship had to change; for "B," they were just fine, thank you. This discussion is, among other things, about the limitations of any single culture—any style—to encompass all that is knowable about God.

All cultures are made by humans, and nothing human can capture the totality of God. Needless to say, we will be working with these ideas throughout the book.

Summary: Style and Theology

The patterns of worship in each of these research churches, although displaying some important similarities, could not be interchanged. One Sunday we walked into the rural church, and an 84-year-old woman was seated at the tracker-action organ, playing old Methodist and Baptist hymn tunes in a honky-tonk style as people gathered for worship. Had we entered the suburban church that same Sunday, we would have found Bach and Mendelssohn, carefully timed to end exactly at 9:30 A.M. In a focus-group interview in the rural church, one man remarked of the music: "We don't do subtle!" The church's style was eclectic, but clearly hymns and choruses with a rock 'n' roll flavor were favorites. On the other hand, the music director in the suburban church stated flatly: "I won't do Christian rock because it simply isn't true!" She had lived through a tragedy that shook the foundations of her faith and found the sunny certainty of much Christian rock too superficial to address it.

Those two contradictory judgments about music illustrate one of the most important dilemmas posed by the research project. How could one style of music be "true," as the music director put it, in one place and not another? A member of a small group of evangelicals who started a more charismatic worship event on Sunday nights in the suburban church confided to me: "The conflict in this church is about Jesus. One group thinks of him as a historical figure, living a long time ago. Another woke up talking to him this morning!" Congregations have unique styles, a blend of their natural past, their social location, their heritage in a religious tradition, and the preferences of their leaders. These styles have religious meaning. *In other words, the central issues in the arguments and discussion about style plaguing congregational life today are theological.* In this book we explain and illustrate just how style and piety are linked, so that these theological issues can be raised for discussion and clarified.

Using This Resource

The conflicts about the nature of our life together are complex and significant, because worship itself, often the crown of the common life of Christians in churches, is both complex and significant. This resource with its accompanying videotape vividly demonstrates both of those qualities. In it are pictures of people worshiping, life stories told by congregants, narratives of events in the life of a congregation of long ago, modern-day people talking about change, and scholars commenting on worship practices. Here you will find history and theology in words and in pictures. We have combined these modes of expression to help congregations understand and work with their common worship practices.

This resource includes descriptions and analyses of three churches. (We retained the names of these churches, but changed the names of the people to insure some measure of confidentiality.) It pictures them at worship. It looks at the faith embedded in their worship and connects it to their life outside the walls of the church. It is descriptive rather than prescriptive. We are comparing styles of worship, not advocating for one as "better" than another.

A videotape accompanies the written text, illustrating through sound and sight the power of differing styles of worship. It shows the three congregations performing the same acts of worship in succession—marching into the sanctuary, hearing the sermon, singing hymns, and so forth. The video shows that these same basic practices of the church can mean very different things when executed in different styles.

In the appendixes, you will find the research project design, including a congregational questionnaire; a selective bibliography about congregational studies and the project churches; and an annotated list of recently published collections of hymns and praise songs. These resources provide congregations with material for further work in the areas covered in the book.

Pastors and lay leaders in local congregations, musicians, worship leaders, worship and music committees, denominational executives, people in seminaries, practical theologians, scholars of cultural history and congregational studies—all will find this resource of value. It pictures the living faith of people worshiping. It provides a theological understanding of the culture of local congregations. Exploring the stylistic dimension of the formation and endurance of worship and religious traditions in general helps to explain why people respond so deeply to changes in music and worship practices.

It provides occasions for people to discuss the most important aspects of their religious lives with people who might disagree with them.

Each section of this resource ends with a series of questions and suggestions for discussion. At some point, a congregation should also view the accompanying videotape of these congregations at worship. We would suggest waiting until after treating the material in chapter 1. Our approach in this book differs from that of many others that look at creeds and belief systems in assessing the religious import of the life of a congregation. We do not deny that these approaches have some validity; however, ours draws attention to the way people practice their faith.

Aesthetic[2] forms, such as hymns and choral anthems, and aesthetic qualities, such as style, disclose the spiritual worlds of a congregation. As a congregant once remarked about her favorite hymn: "It sounds the way following Christ is like." The sounds of that hymn evoke the world of her faith. As we will see in chapter 1, styles of music express central aspects of the religious tradition of a people. It is our hope that you and other members of your congregation will use this resource to explore the religious depths of the aesthetic practices in your church.

The worship in the churches in the study exemplifies only three of the many styles of worship found in our churches today. Many other possibilities are unrepresented in the research project. This limitation should not be a barrier to the use of this resource. Its aim is to do the following:

1. Introduce the idea that a congregation has a culture, or perhaps several cultures. This culture has, as one of its characteristics, a particular way of doing things—a style.

2. Demonstrate through example that these styles carry embedded images of God and of people.

3. Introduce the insight that worship, because it is a human activity, can both exemplify and obstruct the experience of God.

This resource (and particularly the videotape) provides an evocative starting point to get people talking about worship in their church and its relationship to their faith. We hope that it will also provide ways for people to listen to one another as they describe a variety of responses to patterns of worship.

Aids to Discussion

1. What words or phrases would you use to describe your congregation at worship?

2. What biblical passages or hymns come to mind that would characterize your congregation? Sing them; read them aloud. Bring in a painting, photograph, or other art work; or make a collage to illustrate the biblical passages.

3. What examples would you use to describe the faith of your congregation to newcomers?

4. Make a beginning stab at describing the style of your congregation. What is its "feel" or "tone"?

CHAPTER 1

Style and Piety

In the debates about worship within congregations, the word "style" frequently crops up. What do people mean by that word? Ordinarily, when we use the term "style," we are referring to a woman or man who is well dressed. For example, there is a "Style" section in the Sunday *New York Times*, which features pictures of people on the streets of New York wearing the latest fashions—cashmere shawls, leopard-spotted Capri pants, the new shade of lipstick.

But we synagogue- and churchgoers are not arguing about New York fashion trends or the latest hairstyles. We are using the term *style* to refer to something more profound than that. Think for a moment about the hymn "A Mighty Fortress Is Our God," by Martin Luther. The versions of this hymn, as printed in most new mainline denominational hymnals, look virtually identical. However, when sung, the hymn takes on an amazing variety of sounds. It is sung in four-part harmony by Mennonites in Iowa; in an upbeat, unison style of the 16th-century "rhythmic chorale" by some Lutherans in Minneapolis; slowly and with a hint of "sway" at the AME Zion church in Boston. What differs in how the hymn is sung is style. The styles of these renditions reflect the time and place in which the people sing.

Style is an aspect of a congregation's culture. These cultures are "tool kits"[1] of stories, symbols, rituals, patterns of thought, and worldviews with which people build a way of life. Regions of the country are known for these cultures—the frugal Puritan Yankee, the Norwegian bachelor farmers of Minnesotan Garrison Keillor's Lake Wobegon, the laid-back New Ager of California. All of these cultures are influenced by their past, their region, their leaders, and their people. These cultures will have a style. Religious traditions come in various styles. Episcopalians are familiar with stylistic distinctions in their tradition: they label their parishes "high church," "low church," or "broad church." People might say, "I don't want to go to that church. It's too high [or low] for me." Or among Baptists and Methodists in the South, you might hear people say, "That church is not 'down-home' enough [or too 'down-home'] for me." In each of these instances, people are making decisions based on the style of a congregation.

People also have styles. Their living spaces reflect stylistic choices. When people make choices about paint for the walls, where the TV set belongs, what to put on the bookshelves, whether to convert the formal dining room into a room for Mom's souvenir teapot collection, they are making decisions based on their sense of style. Something "fits" in a way something else doesn't. Even ordinary room clutter or the lack of it has something to do with style.

Let's turn for a moment to conventional definitions of style. In general usage, style means the form or manner of an object or event as opposed to its content or subject matter. One might say of a speech: "She certainly was concise!"—meaning that the form in which she delivered her ideas was clear and to the point. She didn't waste words. There weren't many flowery adjectives. In common speech, we often make a distinction between substance and style—between the content of the speech and the way it is delivered. Yet in the discussion of style in the latest *Grove's Dictionary of Music and Musicians* the distinctions between form or manner and content are not so neatly drawn. *Grove's* defines style as "manner, mode of expression, type of presentation" and then says, "[T]o treat of the style of an epoch or culture, one is treating of import, a substantive communication from a society, which is a significant embodiment of the aspirations and inner life of its people." In other words, the manner of presentation of an idea communicates something of significance—the "aspirations and inner life of people." In an essay in *The Question of Style in Philosophy and the Arts*, the philosopher Salim Kemal writes:

> [T]he kind of order we give—our style—is serious and significant because there we make ourselves, display our personalities, our mode of living, our sensitivity to the requirements of a good life, and give as beautiful an order as possible to the material of our lives.[2]

In a six-page handbook on ushering written by a member of Carter Memorial United Methodist Church in the 1950s, we found a wonderful illustration of a congregation's concern for style. According to this writer, ushering in church is a duty, but also an honor. "It is an honor because the usher stands before the community as one representing the highest attributes of the church membership as a group." What follows this statement is a description of the tasks—seating people in the sanctuary, taking the collection, greeting people at the door at the end of the service. It also describes the manner in which these actions are done. In seating the congregation: "With your friendliness, display dignity. Remember, in no way does our sanctuary resemble the scene of a twenty-fifth anniversary class reunion. People should, and most people do, guide their thoughts toward reverence for God and respect for His House of Worship as they approach the sanctuary." The usher is a *model of appropriate behavior* in the sanctuary, a representative of the church. "Carry out your duties with self-assurance. This is not demonstrated by slouching against walls or leaning on chairs. Stand erect. Walk erect. Your position is an honor to you—respect it as you would have others respect it." The manner of ushering teaches people how to approach God. It also indirectly teaches them about God—as One who commands respect and dignity. The worshiper does not greet God with a hearty "How are ya?" as one might hail an old friend at a class reunion. Respectful distance is maintained between the worshiper and God.

This attention to the way things are done conveys a message about the style of the congregation. This church is distinctive because of the solemnity of its gatherings, the erect bearing of its seated parishioners, the careful attention given to any and all physical, public movement within the sanctuary. All of us would recognize our church's style when someone, perhaps a new pastor, departs from "the way things are done." For example, the pastor of the rural church changed the customary way Holy Communion was practiced by adding a simple gesture of touch during the distribution of the bread and cup at the altar rail. However, the addition of touch remarkably altered the "feel" of the ritual. Even though everything was the same except this one small gesture, many voiced their upset about the change.

The Religious Import of Style

As we can see in the handbook on ushering, style is not just a whim or fancy, like the latest width of tie or the cut of lapel on a man's suit. The style of a congregation discloses its inner, collective, spiritual world. It displays people's attitudes about and their understanding of God and people; it also communicates the appropriate relationship between the two. A "church-shopper" senses or intuits this world as he or she enters a church. When people "church-shop," they are reading the stylistic clues given off by the faith community. They say, "This is the place! I feel right at home here."

Here are members of the urban church talking about the style of music in their tradition:

> *A.* The music draws you and it opens your ears. But then music's been a part of black people's lives—for all our lives. How we came through slavery, and the only thing that's changed is the style. Spirituals turned to gospel. The rock music has turned into rock gospel. . . . It speaks of life, everyday life. About putting God in your life. With a beat to it.

The second speaks of the "flavor" of African American Methodism:

> *B.* We have an order of service. We are Methodists, so we have an order of service. But we are African Americans, and so we put that flavor, that innateness into that. We like rhythm, we like power, we like—for lack of a better term—noise, or excitement and emotion. And I'm proud of that. I think for a number of years, African Americans have been somewhat ashamed of that, because that has been thought of being . . . not sophisticated. But I enjoy it. We like music. We like rhythm. And I think we now, our whole race is, it's taken us a while to appreciate that—that we brought it across and work it in. . . . It all comes together, and it's beautiful.

In these conversations, the parishioners talk of their heritage, their racial identification, and their style of music—"that flavor, that innateness"—with its emotional excitement and beat. Making such music on Sunday, they create and enter their collective, spiritual world, which is often under siege during the week.

Style and Piety

Piety is the word that our research team used to refer to that inner, collective, spiritual world we've been discussing. Piety is a much broader concept than belief or doctrine. It includes those aspects of religious life, but others as well. Rather than thinking of religious life as consisting mainly of what we believe or think about God, piety encompasses what people do because of their beliefs: outreach, attendance at prayer meetings, and the like. These actions contain "statements" of belief—or perhaps "pictures" of belief is a better phrase—but in experiences more complex and profound than mere words. For our purposes we focused on the way that these activities revealed the inner spiritual life. We focused on the style of these activities.

Here is the definition we used:

> Piety is the corporate inner life of the church, made visible in its worship, fellowship, and mission. Piety is a function of both reflective and "prereflective" assumptions and commitments about God's being and action, and about the proper shape of the Christian life.

When we say that piety is a function of both reflective and "prereflective" assumptions and commitments, we're emphasizing that the religious realm is often more than verbal reflections, that it lives at a more profound, perhaps unspoken, level for most people. Piety grows out of the depths of people, not just their conscious minds.

In the common, everyday activities of a congregation, style and piety often go hand in hand. The decoration of a church entails a series of stylistic choices. In the many choices available to church members as they choose vessels to hold flowers, colors, and fabrics for sanctuary banners, carpet for halls, and music for anthems, stylistic values come into play. These values must, in some part, be drawn from the world around the church—the secular culture, if you will. The secular culture produces those vases, carpets, and curtains. Members read magazines, work in offices, and shop in stores that show what looks "attractive." These secular stylistic values exist in the culture at large.

But the choices made by church members are not limited only by considerations of what they like, and what is considered conventionally attractive. They must also decide what is *appropriate for a holy place*. What is a fitting expenditure of money and time to decorate a place of worship?

What sorts of emotions should we cultivate in our singing, our furnishings, our speech in the name of God? Not all aspects of one's culture belong within the walls of the church. As our usher reminded his friends, "Remember, in no way does our sanctuary resemble the scene of a twenty-fifth anniversary class reunion." In making decisions about what is appropriate to God's house, people rely not only on style but also on piety. Ideas about God are already at work in the uncountable decisions that go into furnishing and programming a church's life. And once in place, these ideas combine (often spontaneously and without thought) with other objects and events. Such combinations renew traditional ideas or give birth to new ideas about the holy. This is as true of the decision about the paint on the walls as it is about the hymns to be sung.

As another illustration of the interplay of style and piety, let's compare the buildings of the rural and the suburban church. The look and feel of the rural church building could be called "weathered," "lived in," "comfortable." The look and feel of the suburban church building could be called "formal," "dignified," "solemn." In a notable link between building and people, the church's architecture suggests how these people should present themselves in the presence of God on Sunday morning. In the rural church they dress comfortably: open-necked plaid shirts, skirts and blouses, and simple dresses. In the suburban church, people dress up: coats and ties, stockings and heels.

As is true of the music in the two churches (see page 9), the congregations' sense of appropriate dress is also not interchangeable. In the case of our usher, until recently he wore a morning coat when on duty. Had he appeared at the door of the rural church, his dress would signal that some sort of mistake had been made. When you think about it, why should parishioners "look" like their building? There is no doctrine or social rule governing such behavior. The building's style is taken up by the people as they decide how to dress and groom themselves for church. Isn't there a common saying among us, "The people are the church"? Here is a good example.

What we are suggesting here is the intuitive way we make judgments about what "fits" or what is appropriate to church. In a religious context, such as these churches, the "fitting" becomes an emotionally charged topic, for we are making decisions about what is "fitting" before God. Style influences our picture of God, and our picture of God shapes our choice of style, of "fittingness."

Signature Symbols

The wedding of style and piety is a fact of life in each of these congregations. In their worship, signature symbols exist that could be used to distinguish their religious lives from others. These symbols are signatures because the congregation's own piety-laden style is so well displayed in them. They disclose the collective spiritual world of the congregation, the members' understanding of God's world and their place in it. Someone who witnesses the congregation enacting one of the symbols will observe much that is characteristic of and significant for the parish. Often signature symbols are also instances of what we are calling "breakout"—that is, people experiencing the presence of God in their midst. In those moments, the church is filled with spiritual presence. Routinely people carry this symbol-spirit out of the church and into their everyday lives, where vital and sometimes surprising connections are then made. Problems that once seemed overwhelming become manageable.

These symbols gain their meaning in a dynamic rather than a static fashion.[3] Meaning is formed out of a congregation's present-day experience yet is also drawn from members' specific past and the past of their religious tradition. Symbols are filled with past meanings that have formed and shaped the lives of parishioners; but, at the same time, symbols are subject to new meanings arising from their interplay with the congregation's present joys and sorrows. In this way, symbols become personalized. They take on the collective personality of the current congregation.

Song as a Signature Symbol

We can illustrate what we have been discussing by looking at one of the signature symbols of the rural congregation—its favorite hymn, "The King is Coming," by William and Gloria Gaither.[4]

The market place is empty, No more traffic in the streets,
All the builders' tools are silent, No more time to harvest wheat;
Busy housewives cease their labors, In the courtroom no debate,
Work on earth is all suspended, As the King comes thru the gate.

Refrain:
O the King is coming, the King is coming!
I just heard the trumpets sounding, and now His face I see;
O the King is coming, the King is coming!
Praise God, He's coming for me!

The text is filled with everyday images, painting a picture of an emptying world as people run to greet "the King" as he comes through the gate of heaven surrounded by the saints. The music is of the rock 'n' roll idiom, with a refrain repeating the line "The King is coming!" It has a beat and energy that sweep one up and carry one forward. When we asked the people in a focus group to talk about this hymn, they began to talk about Richie, whose favorite it was. One Easter he was playing the guitar and May Jennings was playing the organ before the service began. May described the scene:

> He'd be sitting there, playing the guitar and we came around. . . .
> He'd say, "Let's go, old girl." I loved that. Oh, gosh! And he wanted
> the music loud. His wife said, "He wants it loud," so I would blast.
> He didn't want anything soft. And boy, I'm telling you, there wasn't
> a dry eye in this place.

Richie Comeau plays an important part in the meaning of this song to the people in that focus group, because, as a young man, he contracted cancer and died. In an interview Jim Kelsey related the impact of Richie's dying on his own spiritual journey:

> I remember when I fractured my shoulder, [at] our first youth
> group meeting, down at the hill here, and I ended up going down to
> the hospital, in the emergency room. At the time, Richie was in the
> hospital, you know; he was quite a bit towards the end of his life
> there. And I was feeling kind of down and, you know, pouting,
> "Oh God, look what I've done now!" and kind of whiny. . . . They
> finally got me into a room, waiting for the doctor to come in, and I
> started thinking about Richie upstairs, and all that he had been
> going through, and just how he handled it, and how he was an
> inspiration to everybody. I mean, he was going through so much
> pain. . . . But he was always in a good mood; he'd always tell you

a joke, he'd raise your spirits when you were down, regardless of what he was going through, and I thought about that a lot. And before long, I was kind of laughing at what happened, and all of a sudden all the nurses just started coming in, saying, "What's wrong with that guy in there?" you know! So I had all the nurses coming in to see me, and I just had completely forgotten about what I was going through . . . because I was thinking a lot about Richie. That's the inspiration he was, and I know that God worked in my life, too, so that I would get to know Richie better.

The image of Richie, sitting at the front of the sanctuary before the Easter service, yelling over his shoulder at the 84-year-old woman at the organ behind him to play louder, and the experience of the music-making, evoke in the people of that group the times they had with Richie in which their own lives were transformed. They associate the sound with spiritual transformation and God's love for them, made palpable through the beat and sound of "The King is Coming." When they sing that hymn, they both create and enter their collective, spiritual world. In response to another question, May described that world:

[The Spirit] stands right out and is always there. It just feels like— well, I don't really know. Everyone is always so happy and they sing right out, and they're free to say whatever they want. They love each other, and it's family: you can laugh, and no one looks down their noses, because I'm laughing too loud. I think our actions like that are a testimony that the Holy Spirit is very much alive. That's what my music is about.

Another person chimed in:

It's just something that's there. We love him [God] and he loves us. He's putting that into us.

Summary: Style and Piety

The philosopher Schopenhauer once said, "The style of a man is the physiognomy of the soul."[5] According to one dictionary, physiognomy means "the face; facial features and expression, especially as . . . indicative of character." The style of a congregation's life together is the face of its soul, a vital expression of its character. In the three congregational studies that follow, we will introduce three such "faces" to you. You will learn of the way that they began, something of their present life, and an aspect of their worship life that gives you a good idea of their style and piety. These snapshots of their life are not comprehensive but suggestive. They are written with the aim to illustrate the basic concepts of the book and to help you discover and interpret your own style.

The first study, an essay on the rural church by Joanne Swenson, focuses on the relationship between the style of the rural town and worship in the Community United Methodist Church of Byfield. She shows how a style of worship can both be an event of "breakout" and the cause of "breakdown" in a congregation.

Mark Stamm, author of the second study, focuses on Tenebrae, a service widely celebrated in churches all over the country during Holy Week. He looks at the style of hymnody in the nurture of piety at Carter Memorial United Methodist Church of Needham, a suburban parish not far from the major interstate highway circling Boston. Putting this familiar Maundy Thursday rite within the context of Wesleyan and evangelical liturgical history in America, Stamm discusses the importance of emotion and sentiment in worship within such evangelical traditions as Methodism.

Linda J. Clark, writing the third study, describes the music and worship at Columbus Avenue African Methodist Episcopal Zion Church and shows the relationship between the style of worship and the history of the congregation. She looks at moments of "breakout" and "breakdown" in this urban church.

Aids to Discussion

1. Create a time line of your church. Put the important events and people of your congregation on it. Draw another time line below it and add the important events and people of your town, neighborhood, or region. Tell the story of your congregation.

2. Bring in important artifacts that display the cultures represented in your congregation. You may have banners, photographs, recipes for church suppers, quilts, worship bulletins, directions for worship, Bibles, crosses, favorite hymns, and so forth. Spread these things out on tables and invite everyone to examine them. Describe the culture or cultures found in your congregation.

3. In small groups, talk to one another about your piety. In the whole group, share those aspects of your piety that are common among those in your group. Share some of the differences as well.

4. What would you consider your congregation's signature symbols?

CHAPTER 2

Community United Methodist Church of Byfield

The area surrounding Byfield, Massachusetts, near the Merrimack River border of New Hampshire, was originally settled by Puritans. They established churches of the "Standing Order," Congregational churches whose piety was influenced by their educated clergy, many of whom had attended Harvard University or, occasionally, Yale. But by the early 19th century this area was touched by the religious ferment of the Second Great Awakening. This phenomenon brought to the area a new piety forged by religious enthusiasm and a compelling dedication for Christian witnessing that "ordained" individuals to preach who had not received the classical education of Congregational clergy. This revival had its strongest effects beyond the boundaries of Boston and its Congregational establishment and was spurred by the spiritual zeal of "the sons of Wesley" (that is, the spiritual heirs of John Wesley, the father of Methodism). William D. Bridge, pastor of the Byfield church in 1866–67, gave this account of the introduction of Methodism to Byfield and to its adjacent communities of Newbury and West Newbury.

On the days when this History begins, the Methodist Ministers were known both by their dress and language, their pony and saddle-bags, their well-worn Bible and Hymn Book, and more than all, and better than all else, by their unprecedented success in winning souls to Christ. Under such circumstances, and amid such scenes, The Rev. William French from Sandown, N.H. came to West Newbury in 1827. This visit was in the Spring. He came on business—selling charcoal—if we are rightly informed. He was a man of God, earnest hearted, sincere in piety, devout in conversation and awake to all opportunities for Christian usefulness. The first religious visit that he made was at the home of a Mr. Burrill. He asked the woman of the house if she would like to converse upon the subject of religion. She replied in the affirmative. He entered, they conversed, prayed and parted. Father French spent several days in the neighborhood, visiting the people who received him cordially. He returned home, but visited the place several times during the Summer and Fall, and God blessed the abundant labors of His servant. During the Summer and Fall there was a gracious Revival and a goodly number were converted, and a few still remain to this day.[1]

This small band of Christians established a "meeting" or a "society"—both terms are used in the records—and in 1832 formally incorporated with the name "The First Parish of the M.E. [Methodist Episcopal] Church for the Town of West Newbury and Newbury." They met in a building called the chapel, built in 1831 at the Great Rock, a site that continues to loom large in the imaginations and loyalties of many Byfield Church members.

Up to this time it had had no seats, but stones were brought in, upon which the women could sit, and the men listened to the Preacher from the outside, and looked in through the open window.

By the 1830s the Byfield area's economy was undergoing an important transition. Up to this time the area had been dominated by small farms on which all the work necessary for subsistence took place—what scholars call the Homespun Era. But now those farms were being mechanized, and mills and factories were being established, leading to new opportunities and new sorts of settlers, such as merchants, smithies, and mill owners. To take advantage of the burgeoning population of these newcomers who lived close to the Merrimack River, some Byfield members began to argue that the church should be moved from the Great Rock to a site closer to the mills on the river.

The interest in the Meetings at the "Rock" began to wane, and it was evident that unless a change of some kind was made, the society would go down. It was urged on the part of the Mills people that if the House could be moved up near the Mills Village, men of influence and money would take hold and give vitality and respectability to the meeting; and, as it was no farther for the people of the "Rock" to come up *here* than it was for the people of the village to go *down* there; and if by moving the House, the meeting could be secured to both parties, it was right for them to submit, and the House ought to be moved. But it was said on the part of the people of the "Rock" that, as the House was given for their especial benefit, it should not be moved—so the people became divided and the meeting went down as predicted.[2]

Finally, in 1855 the decision was made: the meetinghouse was moved from the Great Rock to the Mills Village area. When the church was initially gathered at its old location in 1832, a Sabbath school was also formed. Just as the Great Rock continues as an important and living presence from the church's past, so does this school. The Sabbath school (or Sunday school, as it is called today) was established as a separate entity, although it has always been closely linked to the church. In 1853, preceding the move of the church to Mills Village, the Sabbath Day School moved to the village, and took a new name that exemplified its nonsectarian and community focus: "Mills Village Sabbath School Society." According to records from the 1860s, 145 scholars were enrolled, and the society had a library of 300 volumes. In 1994 the Sunday school recorded 143 enrollees, including 60 children, 25 youth, and 40 adults, while the church itself had an average worship attendance of 102. Obviously the Sunday school touched the lives of many far beyond the formal membership rolls of the church.

The Byfield Church Today

In 1994, at the time of our study, the church's pastor was a ministry student in his mid-20s at Boston University School of Theology. Although only licensed (that is, not yet ordained), he had ministerial experience beyond his years as the son of an esteemed and successful United Methodist minister. Fred Cocheran's dedication and warmth contributed to the church's growing from a regular Sunday attendance of 94 to 116 in 1994. The church members' median age was 47; the median year at which a member first began to come to the church was 1980. These dates might mask the fact that founding families of the church still had representatives—vocal representatives—in the congregation, such as the elderly organist May Jennings and several of her kin.

The members' theology was remarkably consistent. Their answers to the questionnaire we distributed among them indicate that they had a fairly liberal Methodist theology, which emphasizes religious tolerance and humanitarian outreach. Their historical evangelical roots were vital: their responses to other questions showed that they valued developing one's spiritual life through prayer and Bible study, and regarded healing, miracles, and the baptism of the Holy Spirit as very important aspects of the church's mission

As for their musical skills, 47 percent read music, 22 percent played musical instruments, and their musical tastes were wide-ranging, with no single category gaining a majority. Rock 'n' roll, however, edged out other categories of music. The congregation rated hymn-singing as the most important, by far, of the musical activities of worship, and thought that any kind of music was appropriate so long as the congregation used it to praise God. In the questions pertaining to style of worship in the questionnaire [see particularly # 28 on p. 124], their roots in the evangelicalism of early Methodism shine through.

Possibilities for conflict emerge in the data about income. Although the median annual income fell in the $20,000 to $40,000 range, 10 percent of those completing the questionnaire made $100,000 or more per year. This high-income group was composed of younger people who were moving into the area and buying new homes built on the farmland around Byfield.

Analysis of the Interviews

The culture of this church was heavily influenced by its origins in a rural community. Not surprising for a small, rural church, "the family" was its dominant metaphor. The church had a homey, come-as-you-are, inclusive style of worship and community life. Here is an example of that sense of family and inclusiveness:

What struck you about what you saw on that videotape?

- Openness.
- Just a general feeling of the whole church, the whole congregation. Open, friendly.

- Everybody feels at home and feels like they're being—you know—they're wanted there, part of the family. That's a big thing here that I enjoy myself. It seemed like one big family here.
- Feeling of non-judgmental attitude, you know; everybody accepts everybody. And we all have our problems in life; we're able to comfort and support each other. We're all instruments. And you know sometimes when we're not really feeling good, it could be something that one of us says to each other, and that could be from God, because we're all spiritual beings.

Describe what you've seen about your worship.

- It's not as formal as some of the others. It's a smaller movement so you can be closer to people, and I tend to think that that closeness really exists.
- It's all-accepting, you know; we're more interested in the people rather than their beliefs, or that their beliefs are all the same.
- The people—it's more of a familial relationship, as opposed to an artificial relationship.

These responses also introduce a profound moral note into this metaphor of family, that of a family in which one possesses inherent worth and an ennobling dignity. This church shapes a way of life with a vibrant sense of God-given dignity, that one's worth before God is intrinsic, indelible, woven into the very core of reality.

In this next section we take up several "snapshots," moments rich with that style and presumption of dignity so distinctive of Byfield. We'll see how this style imbues the church's piety, including a moment of breakout and an instance of breakdown.

Mother's Day: *A Researcher's Account*

As I walk across the lawn, toward the door of the small, white clapboard Byfield United Methodist Church, I feel my high heels sink into the spongy, matted turf. The church's grounds lack evidence of any recent "manicure," as does the entrance to the church: chipped and aging concrete steps with iron handrails devoid of any embellishment, leading up to weatherworn wooden doors opened to let in the sparkling morning sun of Mother's Day.

Just inside those doors, in the small entryway, I can see an aged, tall cabinet, which holds church papers, memorabilia, and other documents of historic value, stored here with little apparent concern for organization or preservation. Indeed, the cabinet is unlocked. Byfield is a congregation with little puffery about its 170-year-old origins.

The open doors are flanked by this morning's greeters, the O'Donovan family, including husband and wife, two preschool daughters, and the family dog, Mops. Little Angela O'Donovan instructs me to pat Mops—how can I refuse? Although they began to visit the church only two months ago, the O'Donovans have already volunteered to serve as greeters. The O'Donovans are not only new to the church: they look new. They are wearing the clothes and bearing of the new exurbanites who are moving to the brand-spanking-new houses being built over Byfield's old farm fields. Rob O'Donovan especially looks different from the rest of the Byfield congregation. He's wearing the summer uniform of the business executive that he is—a crisp khaki suit with a white button-down-collar shirt and striped tie, in high contrast to the sport-shirt casualness of the typical Byfield man.

What drew the O'Donovans and other new exurbanites to the Byfield church? They were seeking to join the spirit of family that enlivened Byfield's social and spiritual life. This was a congregation of sincere, spontaneous caring people, seemingly unburdened by divisions common to other churches, like social rank or professional achievement. This was also a church family whose gatherings were governed more by impulse than by organization, one that featured more uproarious laughter than respectful discussion. The caring and the chaos of the Byfield church made it not only possible but necessary for newcomers to step into important roles.

On this Mother's Day I am seated next to Linda Skelton, simply dressed and groomed, pregnant and obviously approaching her due date. I realize that she and her husband are the couple who had been excitedly discussed during last week's meeting of the nurturing committee. The committee was plotting a baby-gift shower for them, relishing and laughing over the details of who would bring what presents and food, and how the couple could be spirited to the surprise party. The Byfield Church, like a woman's best friend, was a confidant and cheering section for its pregnant members. I experienced this support firsthand because I also was pregnant at the time, and Byfield churchgoers continually asked me about my morning sickness, sent me home from meetings with snacks to eat during my long drive, and teased me about my swelling form.

Here we haven't even begun to worship, formally speaking, but the church's style is already richly perceptible. What have we seen? We've walked on a lawn with no obvious landscaping scheme, entered a church built for utility, greeted people dressed without flair, and noted the worn and neglected features of the church's entry and the haphazard way the church's historic documents are stored. How then can I say that the church's style is so evident, when everything appears to be without style? To an outsider, Byfield's furnishings may seem unremarkable and utilitarian, yet its objects and traditions compose a distinct place, a faith community distinguishable from the neighboring Roman Catholics or Congregationalists. There is, in short, a style or aesthetic that we can identify.

The most encompassing adjective to describe Byfield's style is "lived-in." This church looked like a lived-in home of people with limited income, time, and fashion sense. Visible improvements were being made to this turn-of-the-century building, but they were driven by practicality and crisis, not design pretensions. There was new indoor-outdoor carpet to protect the worn entry flooring, new paint to cover the rain-stained sanctuary ceiling, and a small construction project at the back of the sanctuary for a wheel-chair ramp and a widened entranceway for people with disabilities.

Other features suggested the homeyness of Byfield. It was typical to enter the church and find one or two choir members standing near the organ as the organist played the prelude, humming or singing quietly with the music, just as though a few friends were gathered around the living-room piano, singing in spontaneous pleasure. The cabinet in the entryway that held the church's historical documents was the functional equivalent of the kitchen desk in any home. Homemade decorative objects abounded: glue-gunned felt banners, hand-lettered charts, altar flowers cut from some member's garden and nested in a harvest-gold electric Crockpot. Members dressed casually. The only men wearing ties or sports jackets were those singing in the choir or leading the opening litany. The church was not the place for displaying one's professional status or aspirations. Like a home, it was a place to escape the stressful pecking order of the work world.

Let's look at the connection between this style and Byfield's religious piety by visiting the committee meeting planning Linda's baby shower.

A Nurturing Committee Meeting in Lena's Kitchen

The Nurturing Committee gathers at Lena Outwell's home—a boxy, modest, 1950s-era house a few blocks from the church. We all enter through the back screen door into Lena's kitchen, accompanied by the sounds of committeewomen's children playing in the deliciously warm spring evening. Lena is still wearing her work clothes, white slacks and a pastel tunic with her nursing-school pin attached—her uniform as a home health-care nurse. Her kitchen is crowded with the flotsam of domestic life: less-than-flourishing hanging plants; notes and pictures layered on the refrigerator door, a sink full of unwashed dishes; a large, round kitchen table covered with a vinyl tablecloth; and a saucer of aromatic cat food, placed on the floor next to the table. But who could begrudge this woman her casual approach to housekeeping? Widowed, working, and raising a grandchild alone, she still finds time to be a leader in the congregation. The screen door seems to swing constantly, as the children race outside, then inside to check the action on the living-room TV set. The children get hugs and teasing comments from the other committeewomen arriving. This is a home of the old Byfield—rural, humble, unvarnished but sparkling in its own energetic goodwill.

We finish the details of planning the surprise gift shower, then turn our attention to the regular business of the nurturing committee, the practice of sending greeting cards to members and townspeople. The rest of the meeting is spent going through well-thumbed index cards in a recipe box, each card inscribed with the name of a church member or friend, discussing who should receive greeting cards. The committee keeps track of who has received get-well cards, bon voyage cards, "missed you at church" cards, congratulations on the birth of a grandchild, happy-anniversary cards, and so on. As we discuss all these occasions and celebrations, the meeting becomes saturated with laughter.

Observer's Comment: God's Feminine Strengths

These greeting cards introduce us to an important topic in understanding Byfield—the issue of gender. The women of the nurturing committee were engaged in the religious practice of card-giving, a practice that has long been considered "feminine," in a traditional sense of that word.[3] Even the cards themselves were in a "feminine" style: pastel drawings, depicting sentimental, feathery scenes of children, landscapes, or winsome animals.

What happens when a ministry is considered "feminine," and the physical objects of that ministry—in this case greeting cards—are styled in ways that are also feminine? Inevitably these practices and objects provide the ingredients for composing a picture of God steeped in these feminine attributes. Ministry must be related to an image of God, for ministry is religious practice done in the name of God. That "name" is an image, an intuition of what God is like; we expect continuity between a ministry and its image or intuition about God. One wouldn't expect, for example, a prison ministry to be linked with an image of God as avenging, as punishing and banishing the guilty, even though such descriptions of God are found in Scripture.

Yet the image of God does not necessarily come first, with the ministry following. An understanding of God may come also after we act, after we handle and are influenced by objects we use in our ministry. For example, because the earliest followers of Jesus were Jews, they maintained their practice of celebrating the Passover meal. This practice and its objects provided subsequent material for images of Jesus as the Christ—Jesus as Paschal Lamb and Christ our Passover being two examples. The Passover meal provoked thinking about how Christ provides eternal nourishment through the sacrifice of his earthly and fragile body, just as bread nourishes our bodies through its earthly and decomposable ingredients. In the same way, this feminine ministry of card-giving provides materials that are used in composing a picture of God that is infused with the strengths of the feminine: sentiment-filled, attached, involved in the daily detail of human life, cherishing, holding, celebrating, and mourning. This is a powerful, attractive picture of God, one also found in the Bible. And this is the God we heard about over and over in our discussions with parishioners, in their prayers, in their expectations of how God acts.

Like other images for God, this feminine style is a form of idealization—in this case, a decidedly romantic vision of the way life should be. Two things should be noted here about such idealization. First, these images of a feminine ideal provide a poignant contrast to the realities of the Byfield women's lives. Greeting cards that represent idealizations of family life are sent by committeewomen whose extended families have witnessed the stresses and strains of modern family life: layoffs, money problems, divorce, illness. If the traditional feminine ideal of family life is a stay-at-home mom encircled by loving children and supported by a vigorous, breadwinning husband, almost none of those committee members knew such a life.

Second, this practice of idealization is one of the critical activities of religion. Religious communities concern themselves with ideals, whether it be worshiping Jesus as an ideal for humanity, or carrying out rituals intended to create an ideal human condition, such as being cleansed from sin through rites of confession and absolution. By sending these cards of idealized images, these women are acting as ministers sharing a visual "word," intended to lift hearts and minds to a higher place.

The Church at Prayer

Each Sunday Pastor Fred asks the congregation to call out spontaneously the names and concerns of those who need prayer. Many Protestant churches have such a practice, but never have I seen it carried out with such energy and full participation. Almost immediately someone pipes up from the pew, offering details about a neighbor's surgery, a job loss, a car accident, an anniversary trip. Grade-schoolers and the elderly, couples coaching each other on the details of the problem to be prayed about, the shy, the inarticulate, as well as church leaders—all feel at ease adding a name to the prayer list. And Pastor Fred, like a diligent secretary, quickly writes each of these names and concerns on his bulletin, and then gathers them all into a simple, eloquent prayer, repeating the name and situation, never missing a detail. Usually his petitions are simply, "God, be with ———," simple declarations of our human need for God.

Observer's Comments: Communal Prayer

It is my opinion that prayer was what this congregation did best. The members' homey, spontaneous, familial style did not cultivate professional-level choral singing or complex Christian education programs. But this style culminated in powerful moments of communal prayer. Our research team could see that the congregation at prayer had a special quality of loving focus, a straightforward sincerity as members uttered the names and issues to be prayed about, and an open-mindedness as to what might be God's answer. Indeed, we came to think of the congregational prayer as one of the Byfield Church's signature symbols. Why did the style of this prayer, unfailingly repeated each Sunday, sum up this church's identity?

First, the familial style of the congregation was so apparent in this prayer. Everybody participated. Children's voices and concerns were taken as seriously as those of their elders, meeting no condescending smiles or surprised looks. Indeed, although Pastor Fred acted as an important source of information about members' illnesses and concerns, his role in the prayer seemed to be more the prayerful voice of the congregation than that of an elevated authority. Second, the church's community orientation was vividly shown in the church members' familiarity with their neighbors' troubles and celebrations, offered up for congregational prayer. We have already discussed the community focus of the Sunday school. Now we see this community focus in a religious ritual, prayer. Third, the prayer exemplified the church's style of simplicity in its language, a characteristic lack of embellished or poetic language—just simple requests for God to "help," to "be present," to "heal." Fourth, the church members' enthusiastic participation in this prayer showed that characteristic evangelical confidence in an intervening, even miracle-working God, a picture of God that also emerges in the questionnaire data.

Finally, related to this confidence in God's responsiveness, this prayer moment showed the "feminine" God we've already discussed, a God involved in the details of daily life, caring and attending to events that cannot be the concern of a cosmic God—the anniversary trip, the bad back, the return from a hospital stay, and so on.

In chapter 1 we stated that breakout moments may arise from a congregation's use of its signature symbols. In our next snapshot we'll see a breakout moment coming from this signature symbol of the congregational prayer.

The Mother's Day Prayer

On this Mother's Day, Pastor Fred issues a special invitation to the congregation. He asks worshipers to speak during the prayer the names of women who had mothered or nurtured them. After Fred opens the prayer with a simple declaration of praise to God for our mothers, many people utter the names of women significant to them. In an unrehearsed yet gracefully paced rhythm, worshipers speak the first and last names of their mothers and nurturers in clear, solemn voices: "Mary Edgars," "Cecilia Jameson," "Lucy Barnes," "Martha Mason," and on and on.

The effect of this simple speaking of mothers' names is sublime. The room is hushed—one senses the congregation's being lifted, moving to a new place of insight, yet without any interpretive comments from Pastor Fred. It is apparent that the congregation is experiencing the connection between the love of these mothers and nurturers and the love of God. The moment is dense with verbal and visual references to mothers: mothers' names, spoken by mothers seated next to their young children, elderly mothers speaking the names of mothers now long dead, men's voices with a tremor of suppressed emotion, uttering their mothers' names, all lifted up to a God with many maternal qualities, spoken in a church as comfortable and homey as our mothers' homes: a swinging-screen-door kind of church, easy with the comings and goings not only of family, but also of the beloved "neighborhood."

Observer's Comment: A Church True to Its Style

The insight of this moment? I believe we glimpsed and even felt the profound nearness of God's love, the surprising indwelling of God's redemption in the love of an ordinary mother. What accounts for this moment of breakout, for this sense that the moment was suffused with God's transforming presence? In the introduction we discussed breakout. Let me point out the specific application of the concept of breakout to this moment in Byfield.

First, paradoxically, there is an element of human artistic mastery at work in such times when it appears that the Master is at work in worship. Such remarkable moments of worship are often the outcome of years, if not generations, of a tradition, of an ongoing practice, of learning to communicate within a particular style or artistic language, just as a choir becomes expert at handling Bach's choral music after years of practice and deep immersion in its meanings. Byfield's stylistic mastery of the metaphors and moods of the feminine was an important element in the success of this moment. Byfield had mastered an implicitly feminine language over the course of years, perhaps beginning with the simple claim that their church was "home."

Thus Byfield could work fluently and movingly in this style, painting an integrated picture of God and the life of faith through these images. This moment of worship exhibited an integrity of style, a coherence that canopied over people, prayers, building, music, and movement. "Being true to one's style" is another way to put it. Byfield was being true to its style in this Mother's Day prayer.

Another contributing dynamic to this breakout moment was its medial quality.[4] "Mediality" is our awareness, in the midst of performing a religious activity such as singing a hymn or praying, that *we are being acted upon by God*—that God is acting despite the fact that *we are the actors, we are the performers*. A larger "hand" is augmenting and pushing our mere human work in a remarkable and redemptive direction that we could not have anticipated. In a breakout moment such as this, we sense this medial dynamic. An expansion of meanings "billows up" with layers of transforming ideas, emotions, moral insights, and memories, all deeper than the simple sum of the human actions that went into this moment. A more profound "voice" seems to arise, and this voice is experienced as more than the simple accretion of human voices. That voice, in this religious context, is experienced as God's voice. The insights generated in a medial, breakout moment are experienced as God's message because of the scope of their relevance and their redemptive power. The Mother's Day prayer had such a scope, for every facet of our lives can be touched by the experience of the nearness of God's love in the love of ordinary mothers. And the meanings born from such medial, breakout moments are redemptive. For example, every mother in that sanctuary had her daily labor of mothering infused with new, sacred import. Every person in that sanctuary could realize that God surrounds us like a mother and with mothers, all yearning for us and straining with us that we might fulfill our potential. In such a way, medial breakout moments give us a realization, a feeling, an intuition that promises guidance for the whole of our lives. Yet, strangely, we also are giving—with our prayers, our songs, our actions.

In summary then, this moment of breakout occurred because these crucial elements were in place:

1. The congregation was working with one of its *signature symbols*— creating a powerful moment of communal action, of a community "in concert" (in this case, praying as a congregation).
2. The congregation was working with metaphors with which it was familiar, that it could handle masterfully, that were *true to its style* (in this case, metaphors of mothering).
3. The congregation was willing to be acted upon, to strain beyond these familiar blocks of symbol and style, to undergo new meanings—God's meanings—in that dynamic we call *mediality*.

Having discussed the significance of this feminine, familial style in the life of Byfield, and how it can culminate in an important moment of breakout, let's explore how this style works for two men in the congregation, both facing difficult turning points in their life of faith.

Bob Lund Resigns

Whenever a church member resigns in a huff, there is no one simple reason. While psychological analyses of such church conflicts abound, I have yet to see one that treats style seriously. Here I offer an analysis of the bitter resignation of an active member from the church, emphasizing the breakdown of style.

Bob Lund, a stocky, blunt-spoken man, weathered beyond his 30-something years, came to church meetings in the grass-stained and dusty clothes of his work as a landscaper. I first met him at an evening meeting of the church council, where he was the most vocal participant in expressing reservations about allowing our team of researchers to study the church. I would not see him much after that meeting, for he soon resigned after a blowup with the pastor over an Easter sunrise service that, according to Bob's wife, "was the last straw."

The church had a long tradition of holding an Easter sunrise service on the site of the old church, the Rock. As you will recall from the beginning of this chapter, the Rock represented the oldest layer of the church's history, the 1820s church whose members were humble subsistence farmers. The mill workers who lived down by the river were, in contrast, considered people of means. They began to assert their influence, demanding that the church be moved closer to their own homes. The church nearly died in the ravages of this conflict of class and location, but ultimately the mill workers were victorious. Now, almost 200 years later, this conflict was still playing out: toiling old-timers versus newcomers-of-means, and an old location versus a new location. Bob and other old-timers wanted to continue their tradition of Easter worship at the Rock. But the land was owned by an estranged church member, so Pastor Fred proposed to gather the Easter sunrise worshipers at a new site. Unwilling to give up the old tradition, about eight people, including Bob's family, held their own service at the Rock at the same time that Fred was leading a service at another outdoor site.

This conflict was fed by a prior tangle. Pastor Fred not only came from a clergy family; he had earned a master of business administration at Harvard and worked for a cutting-edge consulting firm before returning to seminary. He was, thus, no novice at finances. But when Fred began to involve himself in the church's financial matters, a responsibility previous pastors had stayed entirely out of, some trustees were exasperated, particularly Bob. Here Bob's wife, Alice, described the conflict:

> When Bob was on [the trustees, the church] wasn't doing that well. And they wanted to spend all sorts of money here and there, and he was saying, "Wait a minute, you've got to think about this. Certain things need to be done first before we put carpets in the church. Certain things need to be done first before we put in a handicapped ramp." . . . The bathroom [at the parsonage] was, like, ready to fall through the ceiling. It was really bad. But they didn't want to do that. "No, let's get rugs in." In other words, dress it up—maybe, in Bob's opinion, to impress people, rather than taking care of the stuff that really needed to be taken care of . . . . It's almost, I want to say, it's Fred's way or no way.

Observer's Comment: Style as Flash Point

This conflict involved an obvious division over matters of style: the style of a church comfortable, lived-in, and practical; resilient against adversity for almost 200 years—versus a dressed-up church making itself presentable for new, more affluent families. But was the church fighting only over style? Just as Bob Lund would not dress up for church meetings, so he insisted that the church not dress up when it still had work to do on the ugly realities of plumbing and ceiling joists. His own priorities about his personal appearance seem to be extended to the church. (As we suggested in chapter 1, members often "look like" their buildings.) As the pastor urged a move to accommodate newcomers, to expand the church's family, Bob Lund must have wondered, "How much prettying up does one have to do for these new family members? Wash the dishes, hide the cat food and put down new carpet?" In Bob's eyes, the church's "come-as-you-are" style and piety were probably being strained. Perhaps he thought: "God accepts and loves me just as I am, grass-stained, weathered, and authentic. But if you change the carpet and paint the sanctuary, does that mean that I also need some sort of improvement to be acceptable before God?" Do you see how issues of style become the flash point of conflict when what is at stake is not simply style, but a picture of God constructed by that style? As we ever-so-subtly alter the style of our church, the picture of God engendered by that style may undergo similar changes, to the distress of parishioners.

Duane Holmes Gets Laid Off

On Martin Luther King Sunday I sit down to interview Duane Holmes, in his late 50s, gray-haired, stout, and gentle-voiced, a beloved leader of the Byfield congregation. I ask him what he recalls from that Sunday's sermon, and as he answers, he mentions almost inadvertently that he has just lost his job.

> DUANE: I'm thinking with the Link House [a halfway house for recovering alcoholics] thing here—missions. I'm unemployed. I was just laid off after 27 years with the company.
> INTERVIEWER: Oh, my gosh!
> DUANE: Yeah, so I just got laid off a week ago Thursday. So, things I didn't have, and I have a severance package, which will get me through a little bit. But I'm thinking, "Gee, you know, I'd like to get involved with that Link House thing. I like helping other people." So, I think putting it all together today, the sermon about Martin Luther King, and that we're all equal—I believe in that. So, it was a very positive sermon to me.

Observer's Comments: A Sense of Dignity

Duane Holmes's comments here illustrate one of the most important features of Byfield's piety: God dignifies each individual. We've already shown how the church's familial, even feminine style provides an atmosphere for a picture of a personal God who cares and intervenes in the small and domestic details of life. Confidence in this personal God gives an energizing, buoyant dignity to Byfield's parishioners. Our research team came to characterize this sensibility as *ontological dignity*: however humble we are by the world's standards, God's love attests to our fundamental dignity. (*Ontological*: related to being or existence.) Our research team saw this sense of dignity in the church members' assumption that, if there were troubles or issues in town, they needed to be about solving them. This dignity is not a sort of entitled pridefulness, or defensive insistence on one's worth, which some people mistakenly call "self-esteem." Rather, what we saw in these church members was a positive civic energy and a sense of ownership that mobilized them to take up important community service. Layoffs, shift work, and underemployment are familiar to this church's breadwinners, as is the anxiety of watching their small-town oasis become subdivided into developments in which they will never be able to afford to live. Yet this small rural congregation knows it is a player in its town.

Lest this emphasis upon dignity lead us to understand the God of Byfield as sober and cautious, we need to emphasize that the continual backdrop of laughter is an important stylistic element in this congregation. You'll recall that the nurturing committee meeting was saturated with laughter. Between the jokes we attended to the business at hand. Other church meetings had a similar decorum. This laughter suggests something about how God is experienced at Byfield. We are known by God with all our ridiculous foibles, but this knowledge does not slay us. God's omniscience is not experienced as awful, penetrating, and judging. Rather, it becomes an occasion to experience our acceptability, our dignity before God. The continual laughter of this congregation could be interpreted as evidence of congregants' belief in a God who sees our comical limits in loving acceptance. God's loving acceptance confers dignity when the rest of the world will not grant it. With such ontological dignity, we can afford to laugh at ourselves.

One of the defining marks of this church's style is the way its members assume their dignity, their inclusion in a "family" that makes decisions and takes responsibility for the affairs of the community. But there seems to be nothing *ontological*, nothing God-given and therefore unshakable about the dignity Bob Lund experienced at the Byfield Church. In his case dignity shows itself to be a fragile creature, dependent upon something as mundane as money: how much one has, and who is in charge of the purse—really not much different from the secular world at all.

Perhaps the style and symbols of Byfield are adequate to convey a dignity that is different enough from the world's dignity, but the symbol-user is not capable of seeing and receiving what the symbols hold. That is, Bob Lund's imaginative vision of "family"—the church's most important metaphor and stylistic feature—was inadequate in this situation. He could not envision how he could be an esteemed "brother" arguing with, yet working alongside, Harvard MBAs and executives from Boston. In the easygoing, laughter-filled, "Mom's kitchen" of this church world, Bob had not perceived how its men lose a fight and then sit down together as brothers at the table.

Duane Holmes seems to find meanings in the symbols and style of the church that are not apparent or accessible to Bob. When the work world told Duane Holmes it no longer needed him, he found in the church a refuge of dignity. Frank Burch Brown, a theologian of the arts, makes this point, arguing that not everyone is endowed with the capacity to grasp the full meaning of the symbols of worship, an inadequacy which he identifies as part of our fallen, or sinful state.[5] When there is some obvious breakdown of the church's style, we must weigh who or what is at fault—the style or the all-too-human users of that style.

Summary: Breakout and Breakdown

There is much strength in Byfield's style and that style's picture of God. God, the laughing, knowing nurturer, whose screen door constantly slams with the comings and goings of her children, energizes and authorizes her people to a ministry of open-hearted service to their town and others. The strong feminine style of this church can lend itself to profound breakout moments, as we saw in the Mother's Day prayer. For some, like Bob Lund, this style may not be able to sustain and redeem in those crises that are particularly painful for men, such as conflicts about money or organizational status. And so we see breakdown born of this style. Yet in the case of Duane Holmes we see triumph, for even when his employer says, "We don't need you here," this church's familial, lived-in, unpolished, and feminine style girds him with an unshakable sense of his dignity and ability to serve.

Aids to Discussion

1. Show the videotape. Note the various reactions in your group. Record and discuss similarities and differences in your responses. Is there one of these churches in which you would be comfortable? One where you would not be comfortable? Why?

2. In small groups, describe the style or styles of your congregation. Find examples both in worship and outside of worship. How do these descriptions relate to the prior session with the various artifacts of your common life?

3. The Byfield church's style could be characterized by the metaphor of "family" and associated metaphors having to do with family homes. Make a list of the metaphors that would describe your church.

4. With the youth of the church, interview the older members of the congregation. Have there been changes in worship over the years? Has the church's style evolved over the years?

5. Describe "breakout" moments and "breakdown" moments in the worship life of your congregation. If possible, link them to the style of worship. In your mind, what leads to these moments?

CHAPTER 3

Carter Memorial United Methodist Church of Needham

Carter Memorial United Methodist Church can trace its roots back to the preaching of the founders of Methodism in the United States. Jesse Lee, Francis Asbury, George Whitefield, and George Pickering at one time or another plied the circuits established in and around Boston in 1792.[1] The Needham circuit covered the area between Boston and Worcester, then a town 30 miles from Boston. Between visits from the circuit rider, people would meet in homes and meetinghouses to pray and study the Bible.[2] In 1832, a church was formed. However, the circuit was maintained, perhaps with a break in the early 1860s, until 1867, when members voted to build a church in Highlandville, a part of present-day Needham and the present site of the church. On September 8, 1867, the pastor gave the following report:

> Our interests at Needham are more prosperous than the most sanguine expected. Few older churches succeed under like circumstances. Our hall is what would be called full. Some are serious and two professed to have found Christ at Camp Meeting. We hope to increase strength and members during Fall and Winter. Members of the church number 25. The afternoon is devoted to the Sunday School.[3]

The establishment of the church in Highlandville was made possible by the immigration to the area of a group of English knitters. A local historian, in the early years of the 20th century, described the coming of these men and their families:

> Highlandville, now Needham Heights, became one of the oldest centers in the knitting industry of this country when a colony of

England knitters was established there early in the 1840's. They were followed by friends, neighbors and relatives in quite rapid succession till Highlandville was almost entirely English in character. They came from neighboring shires, Nottingham, Leicester, and Derby, and in a few decades made for themselves comfortable homes. These early weavers, Stockingers, as they called themselves, were invariably good workmen. They made a good grade of fine woolen stockings for men, women and children.[4]

This historian gives an explanation for their leaving England and provides us with an important glimpse into the culture and values of the early members of this congregation.

It has often been asked, what started this movement to the new country and gave these people sufficient strength and purpose to overcome the obstacles of such a long hard journey from the home country to a totally different climate and environment. Year after year they came, until the sparsely settled village of Highlandville became a thriving and prosperous one, with its church, its school, its store, its Post-Office—yes, and its Temperance Society, too. . . . We have been told that the economic condition of England at that time was such that labor was cheap and food stuffs were scarce and high in price. The adoption of the Corn Laws in 1832 and certain tariff restrictions which also were enacted at that time, served only to enrich the landowners and the manufacturers. There were no free schools in England. There was no chance for poor folks to get an education, or any schooling, unless out of these scant wages, they could send their children to a Dame School with the required pennies clutched in their small hands each week. . . . Had it not been for the Mission Schools, sponsored by the Methodists, the poor would have fared badly in England at that time. Ambitious men and boys (they entirely neglected the girls) were encouraged to attend Sunday Schools, where after the services, they could join classes and be taught to read and write. Many of these newcomers to America had gained some education in this way. . . . Such men as were ambitious enough to learn to read and write under these circumstances wanted to provide better opportunities for their children.[5]

This early experience with poverty and hardship had a great influence on the outlook of these Highlandville knitters. In their new land, they built the church and ran educational programs for their workers. They built homes for them, treating them with what we would now term "enlightened benevolence."

The Needham Church Today

This church is now located in the midst of a prosperous suburb of Boston. At the beginning of 1994, the church had 809 members and constituents. The average attendance at worship was 286. An average of 186 people attended Sunday school: 74 children, 35 youth, and 45 adults. The church had two pastors and several other paid staff, including a music director and a Christian education director. At that time Carter held two somewhat different Sunday services. The first, the one we videotaped, was formal; the second less so, although the two overlapped in content. A third Sunday service, attended by a small but dedicated group of evangelicals, met on Sunday nights.

According to answers to the questionnaire, 65 percent of the people attended the more formal services; the median year they began attending the church was 1968. The average age was 56; fully 67 percent of the congregation had completed college, and 36 percent had a graduate or professional degree. Members' annual incomes ran the gamut from under $10,000 to over $100,000. One of the features that distinguishes this congregation from the other two is its wide diversity of opinion about theology and the nature of the church. No one theological position was dominant.

Carter is a congregation that is musically well-educated: 65 percent read music; 42 percent play musical instruments; 21 percent go to public concerts once a month or more. Its diversity emerges in preferences for musical styles: eclectic would characterize this group. The top two categories are classical/symphonic at 26 percent; and rock 'n' roll at 18 percent. As for congregational singing, 53 percent say they like to sing but don't do it well; 40 percent say they like to sing and do it well. And 47 percent say, "Any kind of music is appropriate, provided that it is done well." Their high standards are reflected in this datum: worship in this church must be done well. The handbook on ushering we described in chapter 1 mirrors this congregation's attention to detail.

Analysis of the Interviews

Carter Memorial's dominant metaphor is the church as kingdom-builder. As a religious community, members are building an alternative to the values of contemporary corporate society, both within the church's walls and in the midst of the town and the wider society. The highest values are personal devotion to God and growth in faith, service, and living out one's "call." The relatively formal and dignified worship at this church promotes individual, inward reflection on what is proclaimed through the sermon and the music, allowing people to hold a wide range of opinions and beliefs. There is a thoughtfulness and seriousness about worship. It is solemn: one's life depends on what is going on here. It is not frivolous or trivial.

Examples from the Interviews

People in worship are engaged in a form of moral scrutiny, applying what they hear in church to the issues they struggle with during the week.

> I think you can get moved by something that happens in the service, whether it be the music or prayer, or words of remembrance of someone. Most of us are out there doing something that calls for a little bit of framework. And if we get a message from the sermon or from the service as a whole that helps us in our daily work, then we feel it was an hour well spent.

> I think people here in this church want to be challenged intellectually by the sermon, and by the music. . . . because it seems to [bring] more validity to your faith. That is, being intellectually challenged and intellectually thought out. Rather than spontaneous.

> I like listening to someone else talk to me, and tell me about life, about what other people think in books, and what the Bible says, and try to put it all together.

> A religious service is supposed to be an uplifting and inspiring thing, in great contrast to what I see in my day-to-day life and on television and so forth. And so it fills a great need for me.

The moral reasoning that takes place is put within the context of the wider community:

> I think sometimes people who are more peripherally involved with this church don't appreciate just how many ways in which it really does make a contribution both to the local community and the larger community, including quite distant communities sometimes. Countries quite a ways from us. People have both the sense that that's really a biblically based expectation, and that we are a privileged community . . . that generates a certain level of responsibility to those who are clearly less well off.

Embedded in the style of this church is a picture of God as a maternal Alpha, whose ever-accepting, compassionate presence provides us with the assurance that we need to strive and reach; and an architect Omega, who constructs an ultimate order of justice in concert with our labor toward personal and civic righteousness.

The Tenebrae Service: *A Researcher's Account*

Tenebrae services[6] exemplify what liturgical scholar Kenneth Stevenson has called "dramatic" piety. Stevenson contrasts "dramatic piety" with "rememorative piety." As he describes it, "In rememorative liturgy certain "events" are celebrated in a vaguely historical fashion, with symbolism attached to each." For instance, "on Palm Sunday, the faithful walk down the Mount of Olives, but there is no donkey."[7] In dramatic piety, the faithful bring the donkey! Dramatic piety attempts to recreate the *conditions* of Holy Week with the expectation that it will reproduce the *experience* related to them.[8] The Tenebrae service, marked by its increasing darkness as each candle is extinguished, provides this sort of dramatic, sensuous experience long beloved by clergy and laity alike. It is observed in congregations in a number of denominations.

Why do we choose to analyze the Tenebrae service at Carter? We believe the stylistic consistency of the hymns offers insight into one key aspect of congregants' piety, the compassion that motivates their missional outreach. All of the hymn tunes and music used throughout the Maundy Thursday service reflect a 19th-century evangelical genre. There are no exceptions to that rule. Indeed, the service has a uniform style that is not characteristic of worship at Carter Memorial. Generally, on Sunday morning, the church makes a wide-ranging use of the multicultural resources available in *The United Methodist Hymnal* (1989), many times using different styles of hymnody within the same service. Such variety is not, however, exhibited in the Maundy Thursday worship. In the perceptive words of one prominent choir member, the music for this service is all "the same" every year.

The testimony of the Carter Church staff gives us our second reason for analyzing this service. After I shared with them my observations about the style of hymnody used for Tenebrae, the staff acknowledged that the annual Maundy Thursday rite is the most significant service in the church's practice of the liturgical year. Furthermore, the staff told us that the Tenebrae has been a set piece at this church for many years, that the musical style of the service predates the arrival of the current, influential choir director, Jeanette Davies (who has served this congregation for more than two decades). For many years, the hymns used in the service did not change at all; indeed, the director was admonished *not* to change them. In recent years, the hymns have changed on occasion, but they remain within the same stylistic family. Nor did the *style* of the service change when Jim Thompson, the pastor who presided at the 1993 service, was appointed to another parish and succeeded by John Summerhill. This rite reflects a time when Needham thought of itself more as a Massachusetts mill town and less as a suburban bedroom community for Boston-area professionals.[9] Such persistence and consistency invited close analysis. It is our conclusion that the 19th-century evangelical hymnody used in this service is a signature symbol, that it provides significant insight into the piety of this suburban congregation.

That Carter Church's most significant service occurs on Maundy Thursday reflects an insight that German liturgical scholar Anton Baumstark (1872-1948) called "the second law of liturgical evolution."[10] This "second law," based on the study of ancient texts, is the idea that "primitive conditions are maintained with greater tenacity in the more sacred seasons of the Liturgical Year." While I think that Baumstark's use of the term "law" is unfortunate—"tendency" is probably a better term—I have observed that many churches invest considerable energy in maintaining and preserving their traditions around Christmas and Easter.[11] Indeed, they often *fight* to maintain such traditions. Even though many congregations in the free-church traditions are not required to use any particular rite or form for worship, their leaders will testify (perhaps with some consternation) that their choices are much more restricted on Christmas Eve, during Holy Week, and on Easter Sunday morning. Congregations have their expectations, especially around these festivals. Woe to the pastor who does not choose "Christ the Lord Is Risen Today" for Easter Sunday morning, not to mention "Up from the Grave He Arose" ("Low in the Grave He Lay"). Comparatively speaking, unpopular hymn choices for Sundays in July and August will cause much less discomfort. The point is that the style of music used during Holy Week often provides a good opportunity for understanding the piety of a local congregation. That most Methodist congregations sing "Up from the Grave He Arose" on Easter morning, while Episcopal congregations do not, provides insight into their respective pieties. Carter Church's use of exclusively 19th-century evangelical hymn tunes during one of its most significant services of the year indicates something important about its understanding of God and the Christian faith. In the succeeding pages, I will describe this understanding.

The Worship Setting

Carter Memorial United Methodist Church occupies a large red brick building on the south side of tree-lined Highland Avenue. Its pillars speak to this church's solid standing in the community. Worshipers turn off the street into a small parking lot, which fills quickly for most services. Generally, members must park on side streets near the church, many of them named after the "saints" of the church. Thus many services begin with a walking conversation among fellow worshipers. After entering a double doorway, churchgoers have a short walk down the hallway to a lobby area with some chairs and plants arranged along the walls. This lobby is always a hub of activity before services, a place to share greetings and perhaps even to hear a little church gossip. From there worshipers enter the sanctuary.

The worship space at Carter Church looks like a formal parlor. The plain, clear-glass windows are adorned with gathered draperies. There is no stained glass. The artificial lighting comes from a series of electric chandeliers. The floor is carpeted. Painted wooden pews are arranged on each side of a long central aisle. At the foot of the aisle is a chancel rail with an opening at the aisle, followed by a short flight of steps. At the top of the steps, to the congregation's left stands the pulpit and to its right, the lectern. Behind pulpit and lectern are choir pews facing each other across a central open space. A permanent altar table stands against the back wall. On the wall hangs a dark red dossal cloth with a large cross suspended from the ceiling.

For the 1993 Tenebrae, the cross was lit, and dark purple hangings were on the pulpit and lectern. A small communion table stood at the foot of the chancel steps. Another table stood in the open area between the choir pews. Its surface, only 18 inches above the floor, was covered with white linens and dotted with several candles. As was usually the case during the year I spent at Carter, I was ushered to my seat. Ushering is a significant role at this church and has been so for at least the past half-century.[12] Through its well-dressed ushers (men and women), the church presents itself to members and visitors, greeting them with a warm yet formal hospitality. Indeed, at Carter Church, most of the men and women wear business clothing. Sports shirts and casual attire may be found among some youth and children but rarely among the adults. Clergy and choir are always vested—clergy in alb and stole and sometimes in cassock and surplice, choir members with gowns and satin collars that form a deep "v" in the back.

Carter Memorial presents the appearance of solid, suburban, middle-class prosperity, and the perception is in many ways quite accurate. Nevertheless, members' lives are not without trouble, unresolved conflicts, and questions that cannot be answered. Parishioners know the stress of rebellious children, discontented spouses, demanding work, and rush-hour traffic. They know tragedy. They have known death, and sometimes it has come much too early. At times, church life liberates and fulfills them, and at other times it brings deep frustration. The membership at Carter is, indeed, a prosperous, well-established group, yet these people are needy in their own way. They come to church—and especially to the Tenebrae service—hoping to find grace that will address that need.

The Maundy Thursday Service

In many ways, the service at Carter Church fulfills the traditional purpose for Holy Thursday—commemorating Christ's institution of the Eucharist—in a manner and style appropriate to evangelical Methodism. That is, the service encourages a personal, emotional experience of the events commemorated; people are encouraged to feel the meaning of the Last Supper and the Passion of Jesus Christ. Indeed, in Methodism there is no escaping this emphasis on feeling. In large part, Methodist identity is rooted in John Wesley's May 24, 1738, experience in a society meeting on Aldersgate Street, London. In that meeting, Wesley heard a reading from Luther's Preface to the Epistle to the Romans. As he described his experience:

> About a quarter before nine, while [the reader] was describing the change which God works in the heart through faith in Christ, I felt my heart strangely warmed. I felt I did trust in Christ, Christ alone for my salvation; and an assurance was given me that he had taken away *my* sins, even *mine*, and saved *me* from the law of sin and death.[13]

That Aldersgate event set a spiritual course for Methodists, one that profoundly affects the church's manner and style of worship. Methodists, as do others from evangelical traditions, often seek a personal, emotional experience of the events commemorated in their services, and often the services are designed to encourage that experience.

The particular tone of this Maundy Thursday service is set in its opening moments. For the introit, the chancel choir uses a Charles Wesley hymn text, "Jesus, Lover of My Soul," sung to a 19th-century evangelical tune, *Martyn*, by Simeon B. Marsh. Significantly, the choir does not use the Welsh tune *Aberystwyth* printed in the 1989 *United Methodist Hymnal* but substitutes this American evangelical tune.[14] In the call to worship, we "gather in the shadow of the cross, sign of God's love" and give thanks "for the compassion of God." In the section "For Confession and Assurance" we pray the collect for Lent, a prayer that focuses on our journey "through the wilderness of this world."[15] In Methodism, our journey (and perhaps "my" journey) always receives primary attention, yet the intention is not selfish.[16] Indeed, in "The Evening Prayer" we ask that we might know and experience God's "compassion and love." True compassion is the experience of the warm heart turned outward in mission and acts of mercy. Again, these opening moments set the tone for the entire evening. The 19th-century evangelical hymnody and the emphasis on personal experience and compassion will recur throughout the service.

The Sermon

Pastor Jim Thompson's sermon, "The Beloved Disciple," is based on John 13:18-25. This sermon is a teaching exercise that helps reveal the meaning of the whole service. It is also part of a series, building upon sermons he has preached at Maundy Thursday services the previous two years. He says, "If you've been here the previous two years, you know about the triclinium." While saying that, he points toward the carpeted area between the choir pews. There stands the table arrangement described earlier (see page 52). That arrangement is "the triclinium." He says that Jesus and his disciples would have used such a table at the Last Supper, that "they were not sitting up at the table, as tradition depicts it."[17]

Thompson reminds the congregation that, two years ago, he preached on Peter, who sat in the servant's seat, yet this servant role was assumed by Jesus, who sat in the host's seat. "Today," he says, "I am preaching on John, the beloved, who sat in the seat reserved for the honored guest." That seating arrangement can be determined, he says, by the fact that John leaned on Jesus' breast.[18] Making the point verbally, he also makes it visually. He moves from the pulpit to the triclinium, and then he reclines—"on the left elbow, like this." Then, he leans back, presumably as John did. He also takes a dramatic approach at one other point in the sermon. Speaking about "the love that John showed," he mentions Jesus' commandment from the cross in which he told John to take care of his mother. Pastor Thompson stretches out his arms, as if on the cross, and with arms shaking and tremulous voice says, "Jesus said, 'John, take care of your mother'" (see John 19:25-27 [paraphrase]).

Why does he make such an intense, dramatic attempt to reconstruct this event? Why does he pay so much attention to the seating arrangements? Indeed, there is no New Testament text that commands Christians to remember the Last Supper. Nevertheless, most people who create Last Supper dramas and preach sermons like Pastor Thompson's insist that they are quite faithful to the biblical text. As they try to reproduce the narrative itself, they hope to receive an experience similar to that felt by the disciples themselves.[19]

The Communion

Pastor Thompson closes the sermon with a prayer and then gives directions for receiving communion. The communion service is rather simple and austere. He says, "We will be receiving communion by intinction [dipping the bread in the grape juice or wine], one of the church's ancient methods." At that point, two young men come to the chancel steps, and each takes a chalice. The pastor takes a single loaf of bread and offers a brief prayer including Jesus' Words of Institution. Following that prayer, he asks the congregation to come forward and receive the elements "as the ushers direct and as you are moved." The abbreviated form of the communion rite indicates that the Holy Eucharist is not the primary reason for this Maundy Thursday gathering. The Tenebrae, with its focus on rehearsing the events of the Last Supper, will be the climax of the service and the essential reason for it.

The Tenebrae Rite

At the conclusion of communion, the participants in the Tenebrae drama rise from the congregation, move forward, and take their places around the triclinium. They recline in the manner that the pastor demonstrated earlier. The candles on the table are lit. Pastor Thompson moves out of sight, taking a seat on a chair behind the pulpit. When all have taken their places, the houselights are turned out. Since the choir is singing from the balcony, only the participants in the drama, the candles, and the table are visible. Both the pastor and the choir are heard, but they are not seen. Our visual attention is focused on the action around the table.

The pastor reads portions from the Scriptures, most of them from John's farewell discourse and passion narrative.[20] After each portion is read, one person extinguishes a candle and leaves the table. Then the choir sings one or two verses of a hymn. This sequence is repeated until six people remain. When Pastor Thompson reads, "Then all the disciples deserted him and fled" (Matt. 26:56; Mark 14:50), all but one of the remaining "disciples" extinguish a candle and move from the table, leaving the man portraying Jesus and one candle. Finally, the pastor reads a passage about Christ's death, the final candle is extinguished, and the Jesus figure leaves. We sit in near-total darkness, with houselights off and no candles lit.

In that darkness, choir member Paul Lockman sings an unaccompanied rendition of "Abide with Me."

> Abide with me; fast falls the eventide;
> the darkness deepens; Lord, with me abide.
> When other helpers fail and comforts flee,
> help of the helpless, O abide with me.[21]

Henry Lyte's text is taken from the Emmaus Road story, when the companions of the unrecognized Christ bid him, "Abide with us: for it toward evening, and the day is far spent" (Luke 24:29 KJV). Of course, people familiar with American evangelical praxis know that this hymn has long been used at funerals, to the extent that it can hardly be thought of apart from that context. The point seems clear—this Tenebrae rite is supposed to feel like a funeral, perhaps even a funeral for Jesus. The devotional style of the hymn tune *Eventide* reinforces that mood.

The other hymns used throughout the Tenebrae rite also encourage this somber mood. They are as follows:

> "Nearer, My God to Thee" (vs. 1), sung to *Bethany* (tune 1856).
> "My Jesus, I Love Thee" (vs. 1), sung to *Gordon* (1876).
> "Were You There?" (vs. 1), sung to a traditional African-American folk tune (undated, first printed in 1899).[22]
> "Beneath the Cross of Jesus" (vs. 1), sung to *St. Christopher* (1881).
> "What Wondrous Love is This?" (vs. 1), sung to a traditional American folk tune first printed in 1840.[23]
> "Who Is He in Yonder Stall?" (vss. 2-3), sung to *Who Is He* (1866).
> "O Love Divine, What Hast Thou Done?" (vs. 1), sung to *Selena* (1850).
> "Savior, Again to Thy Dear Name" (vss. 1-2), sung to *Ellers* (1869).

The stylistic consistency of this hymnody is striking. All of the tunes reflect the conventions of 19th-century evangelical hymnody, although not its rowdy and repetitive camp-meeting tradition. Rather, the best of these hymns reflect what hymnologist Carlton Young calls gospel's "chordal, devotional style."[24] All of these tunes encourage a particular experience of the crucifixion narrative. The music invites one to brood over the events of the Passion, to enter them via one's imagination, and to feel them in an appropriately sorrowful manner.

Two examples illustrate the point. The first is "Nearer, My God, to Thee," a text written by the English hymnwriter Sarah Adams and sung to Lowell Mason's tune *Bethany*.

> Nearer, my God to thee, nearer to thee!
> E'en though it be a cross that raiseth me,
> still all my song shall be, nearer, my God, to thee;
> nearer, my God, to thee, nearer to thee![25]

In this hymn, we pray that God will draw us "nearer," even if we must endure suffering (the cross) to achieve that intimacy.[26] It is an earnest plea for an emotional, personal experience. The association of this hymn with one of the great disasters in English/American history, the ever-intriguing story of the *Titanic*, does much to deepen the impact.[27] The cross depicted in this hymn is a place of cleansing sorrow and grief, not a place of horror and not really a place of triumph.

The second example is Charles Wesley's hymn, "O Love Divine, What Hast Thou Done," which we sang to Isaac Woodbury's tune *Selena*. Wesley's text works at the intersection of the biblical proclamation of Christ's crucifixion and its effect on the life of the individual sinner. As one might expect, the emphasis falls on the individual and his or her experience of Calvary:

> O Love divine, what hast thou done!
> The immortal God hath died for me!
> The Father's co-eternal Son
> bore all my weight upon the tree.
> Th'immortal God for me hath died:
> My Lord, my Love, is crucified![28]

Indeed, "The immortal God has died *for me!*"[29] (emphasis added). The chordal devotional style of *Selena* complements the text.[30] It encourages one to brood over the events, to feel their significance, to receive them in a personal way.

The stylistic consistency of the hymnody used in this Tenebrae service is further illustrated by considering some of the hymns that were not used. For instance, one could make a case for using, on Maundy Thursday or Good Friday, George William Kitchin's hymn "Lift High the Cross," sung to

Crucifer in all its glory.[31] "Lift High" reflects the unmistakably triumphant strains of the Passion narrative offered in John's Gospel. There Jesus is not a defenseless lamb led to the slaughter. When Pilate claims to be in control of events, Jesus tells him, "You would have no power over me if it were not given you from above" (John 19:11). In John there is no cry of desolation, but rather a shout of triumph: "It is finished" (John 19: 29). "Lift High the Cross" reflects those dynamics. Although gaining popularity within United Methodism and other denominations, its text, tempo, and triumphal sound do not fit in most Maundy Thursday or Good Friday services. That is, there is no brooding over those who suffer, and there is little concern for personal emotional experience.

Most notably absent from the Carter Church Tenebrae rite was the sixth-century passion hymn, "Sing, My Tongue, the Glorious Battle,"[32] which *The Book of Common Prayer* instructs Episcopal Church congregations to use in their Good Friday liturgies.[33] For those accustomed to the evangelical tradition of passion hymns, "Sing, My Tongue" is striking for its absence of concern with personal experience or immediate religious feeling. It sounds the theme of the Johannine passion, praising Christ for his triumphant work on the cross:

> Sing, my tongue, the glorious battle,
> sing the ending of the fray;
> now above the cross, the trophy,
> sound the loud triumphant lay:
> tell how Christ, the world's Redeemer,
> as a victim won the day.

The worshiper is not encouraged to feel or do anything in particular, except to sing and give "praise and glory: to the Father and the Son, to th'eternal Spirit."[34] Of course, human experience is not easily divided. All thought contains feeling and all feeling contains thought.[35] Nevertheless, "Sing, My Tongue" does not discuss feelings, nor does it verbalize a personal experience of the Crucifixion. It proclaims the death of Jesus Christ as the saving act of God which stands prior to our experience of the same. As such, "Sing, My Tongue" offers a type of theological proclamation that was missing in the Carter Memorial service.

While some might be tempted to dismiss this Tenebrae service as a sentimental "funeral for Jesus," it is deeply significant in the life of this congregation. Its power is expressed in Pastor Thompson's benediction. After Paul Lockman finishes singing "Abide with Me," the pastor comes out from behind the pulpit, stands before the congregation, and dismisses us by saying, "Behold the love of God. Behold the darkness." He invites us to go forth in that darkness "looking forward to Sunday, and the rising of the Easter light." Indeed, it is an invitation to feel the sufferings of Jesus—the Jesus who was the first to bear the cross, but certainly not the last. It is an invitation to experience Christ's compassion for our own suffering. When a person feels that compassion in a deep and abiding way, he or she is set free to exercise a similar compassion toward others. Such compassion issues forth in Carter's missional, kingdom-building work. Theirs is kingdom building that always remembers its roots in the suffering of Christ, in the biblical narratives of suffering, and in our own stories of pain. That powerful compassion stands at the heart of the Wesleyan evangelical piety expressed in this Tenebrae service.

Earlier in this chapter (see page 50), I mentioned the choir member, who told me after the 1994 service that the Tenebrae hymns used that night were "the same" as those used in 1993. Strictly speaking, they were not the same hymns. However, hearing them, sitting there in the dark on that night in 1994, I might have said that they were exactly the same. In fact, that second year the choir sang several hymns that they had not sung the year before—specifically "Must Jesus Bear the Cross Alone?," "The Old Rugged Cross," "Dear Lord and Father of Mankind," "Day Is Dying in the West," and another solo by Paul Lockman, "'Tis Finished, the Messiah Dies."[36] Indeed, they are different hymns, but "the same" nonetheless.

To what, then, was Fred Martin referring when he said, "They're the same"? He was making a judgment about their musical style. Indeed, the style expressed in those 19th-century evangelical hymns is a signature symbol. It is language from the heart; that is, from the deep recesses of the Carter congregation's piety. This Tenebrae service is a liturgy shaped by the congregation's own situation and needs. For these reasons, this service gains its prominent place in the congregation's life.

Observer's Comment: Relevant or Irrelevant?

Is the style exhibited in the Tenebrae hymns, so drenched in 19th-century piety, relevant to the contemporary work of this congregation? In the introduction to this chapter, we say that Carter's dominant metaphor for church is commonwealth builder or kingdom-of-God builder. In what sense does the Tenebrae service contribute to that identity, which we said is character-ized by a "relatively formal and dignified worship" that "allows for and promotes individual and inward assent to what is proclaimed through the sermon and the music"? Is the style represented in the parish's Tenebrae service an out-of-date remnant of an earlier piety that is no longer relevant to members' spiritual journey? Or, if it remains relevant, in what sense does it contribute to their work of building God's kingdom?

The brooding, deeply introspective hymns sung at Tenebrae fit easily into Carter Church's overall worship style. They also fulfill an important role in members' work as kingdom-of-God builders. How is that? The suf-fering that the congregation reflects upon during its Maundy Thursday ser-vice is not just the suffering of Christ, but it is the worshipers' own suffering and the suffering of their community and world. Such reflection shapes and reinforces the compassion that motivates their missional work. It may not be necessary for the Carter Memorial community to visit these songs every week, but it is important that it does so once a year, in the midst of one of the holiest seasons of the church year.

Observer's Comment: The Focus on Experience

It is difficult to argue with the basic premise of evangelical Christianity, that it is not enough simply to believe this or that doctrine on an intellectual level. Evangelicalism, and therefore Methodism, insists that one must be moved at the level of the will, that the warm heart is necessary to an authentic expression of Christian faith. While all thought contains some degree of feeling (and vice versa), evangelical practice insists that one must *feel* one's convictions, assumptions, and commitments. John Wesley expressed this conviction in his sermon "The Almost Christian."[37] The "almost Christian," he insisted, "[has] a form of godliness" and "does nothing which the gospel forbids."[38] Nevertheless, he or she is not motivated by a deep, abiding sense of God's love. The "altogether Christian," on the other hand, experiences a love that "engrosses the whole heart . . . takes up all the affections . . . fills the entire capacity of the soul . . . and employs the utmost extent of all its faculties." Such divine love moves one to love one's neighbor; that is, to love "every man in the world; every child of his who is 'the Father of the spirits of all flesh.'"[39] I assume that people are drawn to evangelical fellow-ship because they believe in the importance of such an all-encompassing engagement with God. As noted earlier, at its best, such an engagement leads to the love of one's neighbor, a winsome generosity of spirit, deep compassion, and active hospitality. That is, it leads to the type of missional outreach that Carter Church supports. Here we see the promise of the focus on experience.

As United Methodist theologian Don E. Saliers has argued in *The Soul in Paraphrase*, formation of the religious affections is one of the church's essential projects. When he speaks of religious affections, he is referring to those "deep and abiding motives" whose character is rooted in the very contours of the biblical narrative. Among these deeply felt motives are "gratitude, joy, and patterns of repentance, compassion and forgiveness."[40] Religious affections are not, strictly speaking, sudden bursts of ecstasy, no matter how intensely those experiences may be felt. They are not divorced from thought, but rather they are formed and supported by habits of deep, critical reflection.[41]

When the dynamic relation between these religious affections and long-term spiritual formation is not well understood, then evangelical leaders may be tempted to manipulate their congregations. They may attempt to design services that create a short-term emotional response. With that problem in mind, we return to the Aldersgate story and ask this question: Just what, exactly, did John Wesley experience that night of May 24, 1738? We have nothing but his testimony—that his heart was "strangely warmed," that he came to a personal realization of God's forgiveness. We also know that his experience helped energize his evangelistic and missional work. Nevertheless, it remains quite impossible to know exactly what he felt as he sat in that meeting. Unfortunately, the unexamined assumption present in some expressions of 19th-century-style piety is that the new birth is characterized by a sudden, intense experience, and that one can know exactly how that experience feels. Worse, many practitioners of such piety have insisted that such an experience (whatever it is) can be reproduced by using the correct methods.[42]

Does Tenebrae as practiced at Carter Memorial reflect such an erroneous assumption about spiritual experience? If so, it does so subconsciously. It can be argued just as convincingly that the leaders at Carter Church are working at the project of forming Christian affections. Whatever the case may be, the leaders of the church perceive how the events of Christ's passion and death should be experienced. That experience is expressed in the mournful, devotional tones of the hymns they use. However, what if the experience perceived and sought by those leaders is not your own? What if your formation leads you to expect something else? What if you understand the Passion narrative in John's Gospel as a story of triumph, that the biblical text would be better served by "Sing, My Tongue, the Glorious Battle" rather than "Abide with Me"? Here we see a second potential limitation of the focus on experience. If a worshiper is pushed toward an experience that she neither feels nor accepts, then she is apt to feel anger and pain rather than cleansing waves of sadness. Or she might simply decide to continue "shopping" until she finds a worship practice that "fits" her.

Observer's Comment: Various Conclusions about Style

We are simply describing congregations at worship and have not attempted to establish liturgical norms. We insist that one should understand a piety—its true strength and beauty—before one attempts to critique it. A person can gain that understanding only through a sustained period of participant observation, a process that can change a person, as it did me. My first encounter with this Maundy Thursday liturgy, in 1993, left me angry. The service was led competently, and it was offered with great integrity. Nevertheless, it pushed me toward an experience that I did not believe or seek. My second encounter, in 1994, did not bring such a reaction. On the contrary, I realized a deepening respect for the parish's liturgy—even a love of it. What is the difference in the two responses? The primary difference is that I became something of an insider. After my year with this congregation, I came to respect its liturgy as an authentic and appropriate way of hearing the Gospel, even if it is not exactly my own way.

What insight, then, does the Maundy Thursday Tenebrae described in this chapter give us about the piety of the Carter Church people? For them, going to the cross means standing with the suffering Jesus and mourning his death. It is not the whole story of their life together, but it is part of it. The engagement with suffering comforts them in their own afflictions and helps them comfort other people. Theirs is the faith expressed in these words from the Letter to the Hebrews:

> For we do not have a high priest who is unable to sympathize with our weaknesses, but we have one who in every respect has been tested as we are, yet without sin. Let us therefore approach the throne of grace with boldness, so that we may receive mercy and grace to help in time of need. (Heb. 4:15-16).

Aids to Discussion

1. Take another look at the history of your town and your church as you described it in the second session. Plan a historical worship service, perhaps a Founders' Day celebration.

2. List again the signature symbols of your congregation. Is there one service that is central to your worship life together? Describe its spiritual power.

3. Find worship bulletins of your favorite services. Describe to others how they express your faith. List and read aloud the passages from the Bible that appear in all these services. Are there any theological patterns in them? Is God pictured in one dominant way in these Scriptures? Are the people of God pictured in one dominant way?

4. Using these bulletins and the discussions, link the styles of your congregation and its piety. Listen carefully to the similarities and differences among the responses.

5. Plan a hymn-sing of your congregation's favorite hymns.

CHAPTER 4

Columbus Avenue African Methodist Episcopal Zion Church of Boston

One of the founders of the Columbus Avenue African Methodist Episcopal Zion Church, Eliza A. Gardner, an abolitionist and early champion of women's rights,[1] wrote a brief history of its earliest times:

> The A. M. E. Zion Church of Boston was organized June 13, 1838, with seventeen persons who had withdrawn from the communion of the Methodist Episcopal Church, then located on May Street, for more religious freedom and with a desire to become part and parcel of the A. M. E. Zion connection which was manned and controlled by men of their own race.[2]

These congregants applied to the New York Conference of the denomination for a pastor, and the Rev. Jehiel C. Beaman (the spelling varies in accounts) was sent to Boston. In an article on the founding of black churches in Boston published in *Courage and Conscience: Black and White Abolitionists in Boston*, the author underscores the desire on the part of the congregation to extend black control over local church affairs and adds that members also wanted to break with the Methodist Episcopal Church because of that body's ties to the pro-slavery South.[3] This congregation, and others like it, became a center of abolitionist activity in Boston.

> Although the city's five black congregations varied in the degree of their involvement, each participated at some level, serving as a hub for abolitionism within the broader black community. They provided the movement with willing workers, sources of funds, meeting places where tactics and strategies would be planned, forums where issues could be discussed, and a shared world of

belief where black activists could collectively commit (and recommit) themselves to the anti-slavery struggle.[4]

Beaman, an office agent for the Massachusetts Abolition Society and assistant secretary of the American and Foreign Anti-Slavery Society, traveled by train in the upper South in 1844 to witness slavery firsthand.

Although he had been an active abolitionist for over a decade . . . neither his anti-slavery work nor frequent encounters with prejudice had prepared him for what he found. When he crossed the Mason-Dixon line, a feeling of powerlessness swept over him at the sight of his "sisters toiling, pitchfork and rake in hand, under the scorching rays of the sun." Beaman recalled that he cried, then sat in silence as the cars rolled on.[5]

On the eve of the Civil War, roughly two-thirds of the African-Americans in Boston lived on Beacon Hill.[6] In 1866, the AME Zion congregation moved to North Russell Street, to a church building formerly occupied by Boston's First Methodist Episcopal Church. The subsequent years of the 19th century witnessed the migration of middle-class blacks from Beacon Hill to the South End. The North Russell Street congregation followed suit. It purchased the present church home at the corner of Columbus Avenue and Northampton Street for the sum of $59,500. The dedication took place on June 7, 1903. At that point half of its 254 members were migrants from the South.[7]

In comparison to those who remained in the South after the Civil War, the blacks who moved north were by and large city dwellers. They were former slaves from the upper South and possessed an unusually high rate of literacy.[8]

Southern migrants were much more pulled to Boston than pushed out of the South. They came because they had heard that jobs were plentiful, and they chose Boston because family or friends lived there. . . . Kinfolk were the invisible links that extended from the Tidewater to Wheeler St.[9]

These southern migrants created separate neighborhoods in Boston; one of them was located within a 12-square-block area between Tremont

Street and Columbus Avenue.[10] When the AME Zion congregation moved from the West End in 1903, it moved right into the middle of this settlement. By 1912, $28,500 of the church's mortgage was paid off. It had, by then, 600 members.

The Church Today

The membership of this church in May 1994 was 569. Worship attendance on Sunday varied from 100 to 150. There were 17 Methodist class leaders; the membership of the Sunday school, both children and adults, was 36. The median year of initial attendance at the church was 1960. Forty-four percent of those in the church had five or more close friends there. Median age of members was 60. Their diversity shows up in education and income level: 47 percent had an education level of high school or less, 22 percent held graduate or professional degrees. The median annual income lay between $10,000 and $20,000; however, several people were making more than $65,000.

This group was uniform in its understanding of God. Members' evangelical cast showed up in their understanding of the mission of the church: 84 percent put an emphasis on miracles, healing, and the baptism of the Holy Spirit; and 93 percent emphasized the importance of prayer and Bible study. Interestingly, they scored low on "encouraging church members to adhere faithfully to civil laws, even when they disagree with them." We can see the church's abolitionist background right there!

Analysis of the Interviews

This AME Zion's parish's worship is highly ritualized and ordered, and clear hierarchies are established. The pastor occupies a position of honor, and during worship, the altar where both congregation and pastors come to meet God is marked off as holy ground. The worship structure allows for spontaneity, particularly as the service progresses. A strongly expressive and emotional quality permeates the sermon, the praying and the singing. Worship is a combination of 18th-century Methodism and Anglican morning prayer, and the evangelistic service characteristic of American revivalism. The hinge between the more formal style and the spontaneous, evangelistic style occurs about a third of the way through the service, and is marked by the singing of old-style and contemporary gospel music.

Examples from the Interviews

Here is the pastor describing worship and its purpose:

> What do I think about when I'm preparing for worship? I think of order, because the Lord is in his holy temple, and when there's order there, and he gets the glory, he comes before us; his presence is there, he guides the service, and all things are done in order in worship. We have an order of service that we follow, with the hymns, the call to worship, the prayers, all leading, as our former pastor used to say, leading toward the altar stairs up to the presence of God. And when we get to the sermon, we should be at that point, that peak of being in the presence of God, hearing what he has to say to us, and then we come down, to extend an invitation, we come down off the mountain, on the same level as the people, to say to them, "You have that opportunity to come into the fellowship, to accept Jesus Christ as your Lord and Savior."

Here someone describes the music contributing to the movement to the altar at the end:

> Oh, the music is so—so—it goes right through you. You need it for the way we live today. When you're walking down the street, there's so much trouble and hate and everything. When I hear the music, I just feel like running down the aisle myself. It's Negro spirituals, and so wonderful. Our great-great-great-grandfathers and grandmothers had the Negro spirituals, and we have them right in this church here. You know, if you don't tap your feet or sing, something's wrong with you.

The sermon is also a part of this progression:

> I also believe [the call to the altar] comes through the message when the reverend is preaching. I believe the message you receive, you can feel it; you can really feel it in your chest. And they

only don't hear it through the minister; they also hear it through God, and it's time; God is saying that it's time now for you to come home. And sometimes a person has no control, because you don't know what you're going to do. You just get up and you just go.

Over and over, the parishioners talked about the power of the God that they met in worship to support them and their children during the week.

Historically, in slavery, [God] was our escape. But even when we weren't allowed to worship, and we had to stick our head in barrels and everything else, to pray, it was a release. So [with] God, everything that's a problem right now goes away. We focus on God, and it gives us the strength to go on. And that is true right now. It has not changed. Slavery is not the term now, but there are other things that we face. And when I come here, it just seems like all that is gone away, put aside, it doesn't even exist now, and God is the focus. And that helps me to go back. And people wonder sometimes how I can take it. And that's how I can. Hence the power. The power empowers us. So, it all ties in, and it all leads back to our heritage. . . . When you think about it, it's just fantastic that we keep that line right through generation, generation, and generation.

Embedded in worship at this church is an image of God whose first demand is for our passionate conversion, and one who demands our obedient trust and respect. Jesus is experienced as standing beside the worshipers; God is right there, at the altar where they can bring what they cannot tell anyone else, speak to God, and leave their troubles. They are a community. One man spoke of the "connectivity" of the church—the importance of witnessing and being witnessed in this place.

The Altar Call: *A Researcher's Account*

As in the other two churches, style and piety are closely linked at Columbus Avenue. In the remainder of this chapter, I show how the history of a congregation makes an impact on present-day worship. The congregation at Columbus Avenue AME Zion church traces its present worship style back to both John Wesley and the formal worship practices of black Methodism, and also to congregants' ancestors in the slave quarters. As we will see, the two aspects of their style are not easily joined.

Setting the Scene

Columbus Avenue AME Zion Church is located on a busy street corner in Boston's South End. Right across the street is the most famous soul food restaurant in the city. The church building itself, built by a Jewish congregation in the late 19th century, is an imposing red-brick building with vast brown wooden doors. Parishioners pass through these doors into a foyer which leads directly into the social rooms and offices of the church. Their illustrious past is recorded in plaques and pictures on the walls of the rooms and in the corridors leading to the sanctuary. This is a historic, old Boston congregation of which the members are very proud.

Going to worship requires climbing the stairway to the second floor and going through another set of imposing doors. My first Sunday there, the room was filled with golden light streaming through stained-glass windows on either side of the room. At the back is a large window with the Star of David in the center. The "feel" of the room is warm and enclosing: dark brown wooden pews, red carpeting, and the wonderful light. Before worship, people are sitting in the pews chatting quietly with one another. They are very well dressed, the men in suits and ties, the women in fashionable suits or dresses, hats and gloves.

The altar call, one of Columbus Avenue's signature symbols, occurs every week, although many a Sunday goes by without anyone coming to the altar to join the church. Nonetheless, the movement toward the altar structures the worship service, no matter what the conclusion. The purposeful energy of making that trip "into the fold" is the scaffolding for the service. It draws people to the altar. Occasionally the service ends in other ways. Once, the congregation gathered around a woman who was to undergo surgery the following week. A goodly number surrounded her at the altar, while the rest of us stood in the pews, praying for her.

If we return for a moment to the pastor's description of worship, we can see purposeful energy building from end to end:

> We have an order of service that we follow, with the hymns, the
> call to worship, the prayers, all leading, as our former pastor used

to say, *leading toward the altar stairs up to the presence of God*.

The processional begins the movement. The choir and the worship leaders enter, singing a hymn. Young people wearing formal clothes, including white gloves, lead this procession. They move down the aisle. The choirs separate and go to the two choir lofts. The pastors and worship leaders mount the steps and kneel at the highest place in the sanctuary. The more formal part of the service has begun. The service proceeds through several forms of prayer, with hymns, the Gloria Patri, the Apostles' Creed, Scripture lesson, and various musical selections, sung by the Cathedral Choir and the Zionnaires, an old-time gospel choir. Directly after the selections from the choirs comes the time of prayer at the altar, "The Moment of Prayer and Rededication." A member of the congregation describes this point in the service:

> Going up to prayer, going up to the altar, going to the throne of God, moving out from our pews into a hallowed ground: for us going to the altar to kneel is like going to the foot of God, asking for him to bless us and intercede for us. It's an almost closer kind of beseeching. When you go to the altar, it is like you reach out and touch God and grab him by the hand, and say, "Listen to me!" That's very personal.

This prayer time continues as long as someone remains at the altar rail. Background music is played and sung. People move to the altar and away from it in an orderly fashion, occasionally sitting in the front pews, waiting for a space to kneel. It is a worship act whose rhythm and timing are dictated entirely by the parishioners themselves.

What follows this prayer time is more gospel music and then the sermon. Here the pastor speaks of the sermon and the altar call:

> And when we get to the sermon, we should be at that point, *that peak of being in the presence of God*, hearing what he has to say to us. Then we come down, to extend an invitation. *We come down off the mountain, on the same level as the people*, to say to them: "You have that opportunity to come into the fellowship, to accept Jesus Christ as your Lord and Savior."

Pastor Davidson delivers the sermon from notes, but gradually leaves them behind as he becomes more and more engaged in preaching. The congregation is also involved in this sermon, giving feedback and rhythmic responses like "Amen!" and "Preach it, Brother," that escalate in volume, number, and length as the preacher goes on. The sermon builds to "the peak" and, as the congregation sings a hymn, the pastor gives the altar call. This hymn, chosen in the moment by Mr. Phelps, the organist, fits both the theme of the sermon and the energy level of the congregation. At that point, many people are up on their feet, singing and praying. Having gone to the mountaintop, the pastor returns, and bids the congregation to join him at the altar. The bulletin reads:

THE INVITATION TO CHRISTIAN DISCIPLESHIP

The Altar is [the] place for dedication. During the hymn, the Pastor will be there to assist you in the event you desire to make a commitment of your life to Christ and His Church.

As we see in the videotape, a young man makes that trip to the altar. Amid singing, a sinner comes "into the fold." He is immediately surrounded by members of the church, who will help him in the succeeding months to become a member of the church. One interviewee remarks:

The term that we use is an "Invitation to Christian Discipleship," so when [someone is] walking into the fold—[the class leaders surround him] and say, "OK, you've come into the fold, O lost sheep!" and we embrace him. That person is saying, "I've been out there, and now I'm coming in!"

This weekly emphasis in worship on bringing souls to Christ harkens back to this congregation's evangelical roots. "Going on to perfection" is one of the phrases for this process. A parishioner talks about the religious import of the altar call:

In everything we do, there are two ultimate ends. One is for our own souls to be saved and to keep in communication and contact with the Savior, and [two is] to save others and to evangelize. To bring others into the fold of safety—into the fold of Christ—so that becomes a very vital part of the sermon, because the Word of

God is not supposed to go out and come back void. And void means no one has heard it, no one has joined, no one has come with us. So when a person joins, the Word of God has gone out, been heard and his coming [into the fold] fulfills it.

The Music

Along with the preaching, music-making is the most important aspect of this movement to the altar: anthems from the Cathedral Choir, old-time and contemporary gospel music from the Zionnaires and the Agape Choir, spirituals, Baptist and Methodist hymns supplied by the Men's Choir, traditional preludes, postludes, and interludes by Mr. Phelps at the pipe organ, gospel by Mr. Beazley at the grand piano, congregational singing, both from the hymnbook and from the oral tradition—"by heart." And during the service of Holy Communion the first Sunday I came to the church to worship, I heard the congregation sing Anglican chant dating to the days of Thomas Cranmer and John Merbecke, two divines of the early English Reformation. Music-making in this church rehearses its musical history Sunday by Sunday. As one parishioner said, "Keeping the line right through [the] generations."

Many people spoke of the spiritual power of music in worship. Here is a good example:

The Holy Spirit just flows more freely with good music. . . . When the Lord touches and the Holy Spirit is flowing, you get that warm feeling inside, tears come to your eyes, you feel like jumping up and shouting, clapping your hands, and it just seems like once he [the Spirit] grabs ahold through the music, He's got you, he's got you. When the pastor gets up to preach—he's relating on the same basis because the Holy Spirit is still there, and he [the pastor] just takes it out of you a little further, but it's just music can stir you up inside and when it comes to stirring up, the Holy Spirit is just the thing!

In response to this statement, another interviewee cautioned:

Yes, but you've got to have something to get stirred up. I mean everybody cannot get stirred up off of this music, believe me.

If you don't have nothing inside, there's nothing coming out. If you aren't in touch with God or have religion or something, you can forget it! You've got to bend with the Lord; you've got to know what God is all about to get that feeling from within.

In a focus-group interview with the Cathedral Choir, members discussed at length the similarities of and differences between anthems and gospels. The performance focus of an anthem is putting across the text with sincerity. The text does not occupy that much importance in gospel music, because, as one singer put it, "If you miss it the first time, it will come by again." Choir members also referred to the power of gospel music to prepare them to hear the Word of God. The singing of it helped people to put aside their concerns and focus their minds and souls on what the preacher had to say to them.

Two choir members compared the anthems and the gospel music:

A: The words [of anthems] are more specific and more clear than the gospel music words are. They hit a point; they come to a point—whereas gospel repeats so often, everybody [does not have to know] all the words. Now, there are some anthems we can sing every other Sunday, and you will never get all the words. You have to hear the words, understand the words, and know what they mean—[let them] touch you.

B: Gospel is a joyful music. It's joyful! You're not supposed to relax. You're supposed to get in on it. Anthems: you can relax, and get the word, and understand every word. And that's the reason Mr. Phelps always said to us: "Say your words clearly!"

The variety of music in worship serves another function, according to the interviewees. It allows people to enter into worship in different ways. Some people like the hymns, some the anthems, some the gospels.

Conflicts about Style

The tension between worship styles came up in one focus group. People disagreed about whether or not being outwardly active—standing up, clapping, responding vocally to the preacher and the singers—was essential to worship. One person stressed the importance of being "in the Spirit" within a group of people doing the same thing. Another wanted to allow for a diversity of expression, especially the option to sit quietly.

A: I can remember when our church did not have all of the fire that it has now. Back then it was very quiet, and it was very black and very cold, and I used to sit there and wonder, "What are we going to do to liven up this place, because the church is going to die if something doesn't change." And they got some of these fellows from over at the Holy Rollers section of the table [*laughter*], and they fired it up, but we have to thank them.

B: You got rid of some of the old-timers in that same set now—some of the old-timers that strictly wanted to keep it that way. A lot of them went to other places, maybe some of them passed on, and you changed pastors, and that's what brought on the new generation, and they wanted to liven the congregation up.

A: That's true. . . . It took place slowly, but then since Reverend Davidson has been here, it's moving up a little bit more rapidly. . . .

B: The older people that were here that believed in that type of worship—that was the people of the time. The time changed. Those people believed that they could feel just as good as anybody else and have just as much spirit and praising God by just sitting there, keeping quiet. And there are those who do not believe that they can do that. They believe that you can't have the Spirit unless you are emotional, but I do believe that those old people that were there had just as much religion as anybody else.

A: But, I can't disagree . . . but if you've got the Spirit, something'll come out of you. You just can't sit there and be—

B: That's your way of thinking.

A: No, I'm not thinking that—I know that, you know what I'm saying.

B: Well, that's your way you received the Spirit.

A: Because when something hit, it hits you. I mean you don't be playing around, it—believe me—it hit you, and you got to move.

B: No. Some people don't have to. That's—you didn't listen to what I said.

A: That's my Spirit.

B: That's your Spirit, but those old people over there, that was their Spirit, and when they went out of here, they felt just as good as you.

A: I don't think so—

Over the years there have been many conflicts about the style of worship in this congregation. In the quoted interviews, viewpoints follow generational lines for the most part. What one generation sees and experiences as the bearer of the Spirit is judged by the next generation as deadening. Now the congregation reports that the young people find the "fired-up" worship patterns to be laughable. In an interview, someone noted that the very young people look upon aspects of this fired-up worship style as strange.

> *C:* A lot of the kids may laugh at it—it's just someone either really happy or really sad or something like that. But a lot of people think that's all fun and games and stuff. That's why I think a lot of kids got angry when [some started] to laugh at other people. . . . When we were watching the tape today, they were laughing at everything.
>
> *D:* Yeah, the younger generation does see an older person get up, maybe, and shout or jump around, they think it's kind of, you know—
>
> *C:* They don't understand.

At this point in the life of this congregation, the "fired-up" worship style is essential to the religious import of the altar call. Without the spontaneous activity on the part of the people in the pews, the altar call would lose part of its impact. That feeling of being drawn to the altar is generated by all the activity that precedes it. The altar is established as holy ground by the way people enter the room in procession, by the use of the space, by the presence of the pastor and other clergy behind it, and by the nature of congregants' encounter with God there during the "Moment of Prayer and Re-Dedication." Worship centers on the activity of the pastor, but as the service progresses, the spirit moves out into the congregation. True, there is a printed order of worship, but people move through it at their own pace. At times the pastor controls the movement of the service; at other times the congregation does. For example, on one very hot July day, one of the lead singers in the Zionnaires took the microphone and started an improvised, chanted dialogue in song with Mr. Beazley at the piano. Up to that point, the service had lagged along in the 90-degree heat; at the end of this dialogue, the place was filled with spirit. This action was not in the bulletin, nor did the pastor cue the choir member. The singer felt a need and acted on it. This kind of leadership is not unusual. Often, in the latter stages of worship, songs are raised from the congregation, and people feel free to stand up and start praying aloud.

The freedom to move and to begin acts of worship coupled with the amount of energy and emotion flowing in the room at the end of the pastor's sermon make that movement to the altar easier to do. Someone remarked, "You just go! You're halfway down that aisle before you wake up to what you are doing!" The "fired-up" style of worship aids in giving oneself to God. If it were replaced by a more formal and subdued style, something essential to the piety of the congregation would be lost. Does that mean that any altar call requires this style of worship? Not necessarily, but in this congregation at this time, it does.

Not everyone in the congregation is comfortable with this style of worship. Here is one interviewee's comment about gospel music:

> I'm somewhat unorthodox when you come to this kind of question. [In gospel music] there is not enough depth in theology. Therefore a lot of feeling comes in, you see. And I know that "seeing is believing," and "feeling is the naked truth." But you've got to be kind of studied in [what is] sound and profound [theology] in order not to be carried away with that kind of emotional thrust. Because it takes thinking away. You cannot be too emotional and think critically at the same time.

Controversy about the fired-up style of worship is not new to the more formal worship styles of historic black Methodism. Daniel Payne, a bishop of the African Methodist Episcopal Church and an important figure in the 19th century, made the following disdainful comments in his *Recollections of Seventy Years* (Nashville, 1888), about one of the current, rather flamboyant worship practices, the "ring shout."

> After the sermon, they formed a ring, and, with coats off, sung, clapped their hands and stamped their feet in a most ridiculous and heathenish way. I requested the pastor to go and stop their dancing. At his request, they stopped their dancing and clapping of hands, but remained singing and rocking their bodies to and fro. . . . After the sermon in the afternoon, having another opportunity of speaking alone to this young leader of the singing and clapping ring, he said: "Sinners won't get converted unless there is a Ring. . . . The Spirit of God works upon people in different ways. . . ."[11]

Popular religious practices, though certainly not the dance, gradually seeped into the formal worship practices of the 19th-century black Methodist churches, but not without great controversy. The tensions between the urban North and the rural South, between generations, and between more formally educated and less formally educated people fueled the controversy.

Observer's Comments: Stylistic Uneasiness

Being an Episcopalian and a classically trained organist, I was in new territory when I started worshiping in this church. I found the "fired-up" style exhilarating. I loved all the old-time hymns and the gospel music. I particularly enjoyed the mixture of the music. Because the music leaders drew music from so many sources, many of them familiar to me, I could join in immediately. The communion service, rooted in 18th-century Anglicanism, was also familiar to me, although their way of singing the chant was nothing like the way I learned it in the "low-church" Episcopalianism of my youth. Just the fact that they were singing this chant helped me to feel more at home.

Having said that, I was never tempted to answer the altar call. Of course, this particular call was closely linked to joining the church and, since I was there as a researcher, responding to it would have been inappropriate. I was tempted to take part in the "Moment of Prayer and Rededication" but felt self-conscious doing it, again because of my role as a researcher. In other words, I never wholeheartedly joined in the "fired-up" worship patterns, although the music and the preaching drew me as they must have drawn others who got up out of their pews and went to the altar. Was it because of my status as a researcher that I had such reactions, or was there something about the style that put me off?

I have a suspicion of groups of people engulfed in feeling, ingrained in me during my growing-up years in the Second World War. The American people were caught up in war. Movies, newspapers, and radio broadcasts molded us into a cohesive support system for the fighting force overseas. Images of the large Nazi rallies in open squares with jackbooted soldiers marching in precision haunted my sleep. Posters of Uncle Sam and songs on the radio about Hitler and Mussolini filled our towns. No one could make the sacrifices demanded of us without rallying cries and the molding of fervor. True, the strong feelings occasionally spilled over into anti-German and anti-Japanese hysteria— internment camps and open hostility against Americans who were "different"—but we excused these outbursts as the necessity of war.

Fifty years later, I am still uneasy in groups of people awash in strong feeling. I resist being molded, even in such holy ways as an altar call. I did develop a way to participate in the altar call at Columbus Avenue, given my unusual position. I welcomed the fervor of other people in the sanctuary, letting it stimulate my own need for prayer. Praying in that church was not like any other praying I have done, before or since.

During the project, I found other people in this congregation who also voiced discomfort with the style. It did not "fit" everyone who came to worship regularly. Yet they were there, Sunday after Sunday. The piety expressed in the altar call was broad enough to include those who did not actually take part in the *actions* of worship but were caught up in its *spirit*.

What would I have said had I been a part of the argument about style in that focus group I quoted at length on page 75? I think that I would have gone with the Holy Roller side, provided that these folk understood that their *way of knowing is* a *way of thinking* and that other people may have a different way of knowing and thinking. Being who I am, I would have been uncomfortable in any situation in which my religious experience was compelled to move in a certain direction—where I would be judged as "not Christian enough" if, week after week, I sat in the pew rather than going to the altar. I never felt that compulsion at Columbus Avenue Church. I do not know how others felt.

The skill of Pastor Davidson and the other worship leaders allowed such broad participation to take place. They were comfortable in these forms; the many choirs and the organist and pianist provided a contrast. The pastor's sermons, although certainly fired-up, were biblically based and carefully thought through. The length and the leisurely pace of worship also helped to incorporate all these styles.

The Limits of Styles

The spontaneous reaction so common at Columbus Avenue was duplicated in one place in the worship service we taped at the Byfield church. During the singing of "Lord of the Dance," a parishioner stood up and started dancing. She had participated in worship with movement in it at a United

Methodist annual conference that year and took this opportunity to try to get her more staid friends back home to show a little spirit. They let *her* do it, but didn't respond similarly. In the meeting where we showed the video-tape to the Byfield church, much characteristic laughter erupted at her spontaneous act. And although there was a value put on the spontaneous parts of the service in the Byfield church, there were limits. In one of the focus group interviews, a group member said about raising one's hands in the middle of worship:

> I think that I would feel a little bit threatened perhaps, if everyone started to raise them. Because I don't necessarily feel moved to do that. I'm comfortable with it at the level that it's at right now, but if it became much more exuberant, if there's much more acting out. . . . Not that I think it's wrong.

So the more informal style of worship at the Byfield church had its limits. Not surprisingly, Columbus Avenue's style had its limits, too. I asked Pastor Davidson what those limits might be for the present congregation. He immediately retorted, "The drum!" There were people in his congregation who went to a more freewheeling church on Sunday afternoons—one with a small combo with drums. They wanted that style of music at their church home. However, the pastor knew that he would get lots of negative feedback from some members if the drum were introduced in worship, so he was moving slowly on the drum issue.

Who or what sets these limits? The characteristic style of a congregation sets them. Too much movement in another, different direction makes the style no longer recognizable. How much added sugar does it take before salt has lost its savor? The same thing happens to the styles that we inhabit. We bring them with us wherever we go. Things we do make sense within them. Our signature symbols are filled with them. I brought my northern Ohio Episcopalianism with me to Columbus Avenue Church, along with my upbringing during the Second World War. Even after 50 years, I am still uneasy in the midst of emotionally charged crowds.

However, the desire to move beyond the limits of a particular style was evident in each of these congregations, too. Back in the 19th century, the young preacher told Bishop Payne, "The Spirit of God works upon people in different ways." Bishop Payne considered many of the ways he had just witnessed to be heathenish. In a conference on worship in the AME Zion connection in 1998, a young 20th-century preacher told about the youth wanting to include rap music in worship. Many people were opposed to it, including those who had in the past fought to include gospel music in their Sunday morning worship. But I have an idea that in youth groups all over the country, people are writing hymns with a rap beat to them. As one parishioner said:

> Music's been a part of black people's lives—for all our lives. How we came through slavery, and the only thing that's changed is the style. Spirituals turned to gospel. The rock music has turned into rock gospel. . . . It speaks of life, everyday life. About putting God in your life. With a beat to it.

Style is the "face" of young people's souls, too. World War II is ancient history to them. Spirituals, gospels, rock, rock gospel—and rap? What music will accompany their walk "into the fold" in the future?

Aids to Discussion

1. Interview a few of the young people on their ideas about worship. Join the youth group to plan worship for the congregation.

2. Break up into small groups consisting of people with a range of opinions. "Paint" a verbal picture of your style. What are the strengths, as you see them, to the style of worship in your church? What are its limits? Where are the divisions in your congregation on the matter of style?

3. In those same small groups, plan a 15-minute prayer service for yourselves and others. What is retained from the style that you have mastered? What is cast aside? At the close of the meeting, use one of these services for a final prayer time.

4. Take up again your discussion of "breakout" and "breakdown" in light of your prayer services. Do they help you to see both the limits and the strengths of your style?

CHAPTER 5

Exploring Worship Style

In the last three chapters, we encountered three congregations. We learned a bit about their history and who they are in the present. We learned about their worship lives and their faith lives. We looked at them through two lenses—style and piety. In each of these congregations, style displays profound and complex aspects of its communal faith life. Rather than an artificial or trivial aspect of worship, style goes right to the core of it.

What have we noted? The activities of a congregation often borrow from the style of its cultural context. Worship, too, shares this style but in a limited way. Some aspects of a cultural style are appropriate for the sanctuary of a church, and others are not. What kind of behavior is fit and seemly in the worship space of the church? What is appropriate behavior for a member of this congregation? Distinguishing between behavior that is fit or unfit for church has wider cultural implications. When the minister comes to our homes, we adopt patterns of behavior related to our "church-going" style. The good teacups are hauled out and washed; the house is given an extra dusting; Grandma's famous apple pie comes piping hot out of the oven. In other words, in the borrowing process, aspects of a cultural style become hallowed through association with the sacred.

A congregation's style displays its collective inner life and aspirations. It is the face of its soul, to paraphrase the German philosopher Arthur Schopenhauer (1788–1860). The informal energy of the Byfield church's worship surrounds newcomers as they step into the entrance hall. Amid the busy buzzing of the pre-service singing and milling around, the ushers greet new worshipers like long-lost friends. "Come in, come in! Everyone's welcome." Not only are they displaying their basic friendliness in this greeting; they are drawing people into a journey with God, a form of lifelong sanctification. In their embracing warmth, they offer help along the way: support, nourishment, laughter, tears.

We also noted that styles are steeped in the past. Each congregation's founding narrative lives on in its piety. For example, in Byfield, the conflict between the "mill villagers" and the "people of the Rock" remains. The worship space of a congregation is also a prominent and visible embodiment of that past: the way the pews or seats are arranged, the placement of the pulpit, the altar or table, the furnishings, the stained-glass windows containing the names of former pastors and loved ones. Entering the sanctuary on Sunday morning, people walk into their past. Sitting in a pew, people revisit past events in their mind's eye, reconnecting with important saints of the community. Worship services are also filled with the past. Columbus Avenue displays its past in the recapitulation of the musical styles of its history: anthems, spirituals, gospels, Wesley and Isaac Watts hymns, and Anglican chant. In Tenebrae during Holy Week, people at Carter Church dramatize the last events of Jesus' life on earth, interpreting the meaning of those days through their hymnody. This congregation uses a devotional style of music from the 19th century to clothe the well-known words and actions of Jesus— a story that is 20 centuries old.

Even the most contemporary of services borrows from the past. It is inescapable. When Scripture is read, when prayers are prayed, when sermons are preached or dramatized, worship leaders are working with forms handed down to them by that vast "cloud of witnesses" on whose invisible shoulders they stand.

A style also holds clues to the future of a congregation because it displays its aspirations—what it works to become. In the rural church, the congregants' invitation to newcomers to journey with them comes with a goal in mind. A future is described in their style, one in which everyone has dignity in the eyes of God. The suburban church, too, is building a future as a community filled with justice and peace. Members take the same skills that they have developed in the workplace to construct an alternative world. The entrepreneurial spirit honed in businesses up and down Boston's high-tech corridor undergirds the construction of schools for their children, shelters for the homeless, mission projects in Honduras. In the urban church, the conflict about "fired-up" worship is about the future as well as the past. Change is promoted in the name of young people, to draw them into worship that seems more congenial to them. People said: "This church is going to die if something doesn't change." The "fired-up" style is a promise to the young people in that congregation that what happens here has everything to do with them, their hopes and dreams.

We noted that any style has the capacity to be the medium for the Spirit, a medial, breakout moment. In each of these congregations, its style comes vividly alive in its signature symbols—altar call, Mother's Day prayer, Tenebrae. Yet we also saw the limitations of these styles. Styles by their nature cannot adequately plumb the mystery of God. They lay out one path to God and, in so doing, bypass others. They break down, unable to hold people together in conflict. They lose their creative juices.

Styles are not interchangeable. What fits in one congregation does not go well in another. If the music programs of these three congregations were interchanged, an essential aspect of the piety of these communities would be lost. Think for a minute of the contrast between a congregation in a predominantly white suburb and a congregation in a predominantly black urban neighborhood singing the spiritual "Let My People Go." Ostensibly the subject matter is the same in both instances, yet the style of singing so changes what is sung that the two "singings" have divergent meanings. The contrast in style comes mainly from two interrelated factors: (1) the difference in the relationship between the text and the piety of the singers, and (2) the singing traditions of the two communities. The immediacy of the cry "Let my people go" is reinforced by the past legacy of those communities that trace their ancestry back to the slave quarters that gave birth to the spirituals. That past, handed down in the improvisational quality of singing that evokes the drum in its rhythms and melodic complexity, is re-appropriated by every generation in the style of its singing. This singing tradition shapes the event by linking the faith and endurance of the slave to the contemporary African American confronting the racism of American society. In a predominantly white community, the spiritual takes on a broader connotation. It speaks of liberation, but lacks the specific reference to the history of a community. It also lacks the improvisational quality that is so essential to a spiritual's rhythmic intensity.

What would happen if the improvisational style of singing among African Americans was lost? A similar question might be asked about any congregational style. The loss of these traditional styles means the loss of an aspect of a congregation's piety. Choir practice, congregational rehearsals of hymns and choruses, and other times of music education go on in churches partly to guarantee the endurance of musical traditions that express their soul. In a Mennonite church we visited in Iowa, the children are routinely excused for the last 20 minutes of worship to go to music class, where they learn the four-part *a cappella* singing style so central to that congregation's life together. What is true of singing styles can also be true of praying styles. Going back to the comments made about Byfield's style of praying (page 34), people there have so mastered it over years of worship attendance that they live through it. Even the children feel competent in using it. Take away the style of praying, or replace it with a prayer read from a book by the pastor with no input by the congregation, and something invaluable would be lost.

If styles are not interchangeable, then it follows that they are not identical. Each style has its own character, its own meaning. What may be achieved in one style may be lacking in another. The more formal style of the suburban church leads to a meditative posture before God that is lost in the hubbub of the rural church. The power and excitement of the altar call at the end of worship at the urban church does not allow for those last few quiet words spoken to God in the suburban church.

Changing Styles

As we all know, though, there are times when these styles that are so dear to all of us must change. Why? Styles change because pieties change: people are led into new paths by God. For example, missionaries return to the community that sent them out and find that the style that worked so nicely in the past has developed some tight, constricting places now. Their piety, honed in the mission field, no longer belongs in the old style. Something has to give. However, worshipers do not need to travel out of their familiar worship home to experience dramatic changes in their relationship to God. Within the familiar style itself, people in congregations experience dramatic changes in their understanding of God. It is paradoxical that the very style that serves the old piety can also be the initiator of the new. Familiar hymns, the words of the Lord's Prayer, the cross on the altar—these icons of our faith can suddenly take on a shimmer of new meaning as they transform the experiences we bring with us to worship. A person coming into the church for the memorial service of a young friend sees the cross over the altar in a completely new way, setting her off on a new path in her faith journey.

The necessity for change also grows out of fluctuations and shifts in our society. Many sociologists, Robert Wuthnow being the most prolific and well known, have described and documented changes among American church- and synagogue-goers in the last 50 years. Attendance in what used to be called "mainline" Protestantism is declining. Stable cities and towns that supported these churches are now filled with people who move in and then, two years later, move out to the next town or the next state. The economic boom of the last decade has accelerated this destabilizing process. Scholars also document a decline in denominational loyalty. On December 7, 1997, the *New York Times Magazine* ran a special issue, "God Decentralized." On the front page its editors wrote, "Americans are still among the most religious people on the planet. But these days, they're busy inventing unorthodox ways to get where they're going." All you have to do is read the issue's table of contents to know that things are changing. Spiritual practices today come in every form imaginable, and they do not necessarily take place in church buildings or synagogues.

Because of the transient nature of today's world, there is no guarantee that the people who visit your congregation for the first time on the Sabbath or on Sunday morning will have much in common with the people who are there regularly. They are not in on the past-saturated meaning of a congregation's signature symbols. They may recognize something of what you are doing but will need guidance to understand its deeper meaning. Even in the relatively stable and historic congregations featured in this project, conflicts existed, growing in some measure out of the multiplicity of cultures represented. What then? Short of turning away all those who do not "fit" a particular style, congregations need to make some kind of accommodation to this multiplicity to retain the people who come through their doors. But beyond the "numbers game," there is a more compelling and profound reason for undertaking change. The spiritual health of a congregation's soul demands it. Roadblocks to God appear when a congregation uses its style to cast yesterday's piety into stone. It carves the modern equivalent of the Golden Calf, making an idol of what worked in the past.

The best description and analysis of this all-too-human tendency toward idolatry comes from the theologian Henry Wieman. In his book *The Source of Human Good* he makes a distinction between *creative* good and *created* good. The former has a yeasty, dynamic, God-laden quality. It is the *source* of the created good. Here he describes an event of creative good:

> [In such an event] a process of reorganization is going on, generating new meanings, integrating them with the old, endowing each

event as it occurs with a wider range of reference, molding the life
of a [person] into a more deeply unified totality of meaning.[1]

As an illustration of such creative good, let's return to the story of Jim
and Richie in the hospital and "The King is Coming." Layers and layers of
good times and faith transformation are crowded around that hymn for the
Byfield congregation. Its power to generate good still lives; Jim's recall of
Richie singing that hymn transforms a situation, bringing good out of what at
first looked like total disaster. What went on in that hospital room was a
change of heart, despite the negative state of Jim's mind. It was an example
of religious transformation. Remembering singing with Richie brought back
the powerful experience, so that once again, the creative good enlivened
people.

However, as Wieman points out, when the "created good" is used to
block or draw attention away from the generative quality of the "creative
good," it becomes a barrier to transformation. "The gravest peril that [people]
have to face resides in the way . . . created good can arouse an absolute-
ness and supremacy of loyalty which only its source, creative good, the
generating event, really commands."[2] Congregations risk such a danger
when they refuse to allow anything to change. They want worship to keep
producing the same exact experience over and over. Under such a demand,
the routines of worship become stale and lifeless, because they are her-
metically sealed off from the lives of the parishioners whose lives change
daily. (Ironically it is often the parishioners who are most adamant about not
changing things!) The sermons the pastor preaches begin to sound the same—
the same jokes, the same anecdotes, the same themes. The choir rehashes
the same anthems year in, year out, and the congregation sings the same 20
hymns. This idolatry of the "known" exists across the board, no matter
what the style or claim to spontaneity. Contemporary worship planners sometimes demand the same loyalty to the spontaneous circumstances that created that first "worship high." The spontaneity then becomes routine, its
capacity to create good—its true creativity—blocked. Simply repeating what
was a "hit" in bygone times until attendance dwindles to nothing is a good
sign that the generative good of the initial event has died.

Each of the congregations in this study was faced with this temptation.
Indeed, worship leaders in all religious communities work with the tension
between the familiar and the new all the time, since worship includes, indeed requires, some form of repetition. The forms and patterns of worship

are centuries old. Their familiarity is one reason that they are frequently instances of what Wieman would call "the creative good." Worshipers can delve more deeply into these age-old patterns because they are no longer caught up with the surface. As we have seen in the three churches studied, the depth of their signature symbols is unlocked through repetition, which allows for mastery to grow. Even the children become users of these symbols. And where would we be without the Lord's Prayer, one of the most repeated acts of worship in the world?

Worship scholars use the word *anamnesis* to get at the capacity of rituals to be generative of the creative good. What is meant by that term? In Christian baptism, we do not simply *think* back to the baptism of Jesus in the River Jordan. In the midst of the water, the squirming children, the hovering parents and godparents, and the familiar words, Jesus joins us. These ancient actions are medial events. We enact them, but God acts in them, too. In baptism, the child or the convert enters the community: not only is meaning widened and deepened for the one baptized; the community is also changed in the welcoming of this new life. So repetition isn't the culprit, but rather the use of repetition in an idolatrous fashion that would block the good. For example, what would happen if the style of Tenebrae at Carter Church became standard practice on ordinary Sundays? In its place during Holy Week, it powerfully undergirds the missional stance of the congregation. Yet the music on Sunday mornings, taken from many eras, cultures, and traditions, serves the congregation's goals to reach beyond its walls to mission sites in its neighborhood and the wider world. Together these styles serve the broader purposes of the congregation. Clinging to that devotional style of 19th-century hymnody would spell death to the broader piety of the congregation. Yet its judicious use is essential and powerful.

New hymns, new patterns of gathering, new instruments, new people provide a sterling opportunity for the "creative good." Many Jewish and Christian traditions and denominations have made significant changes in their worship patterns over the last 40 years, spurred on by the Second Vatican Council, which launched a momentous process of worship renewal in the Roman Catholic Church. With these changes has come renewed commitment to mission, to the stranger outside the door, to the people who have been outsiders, to the oppressed and the marginalized. The worldwide evangelical movement brings to prominence lively styles of worship, as it also turns our attention to the necessity for evangelism. A glance at the new hymnals, worship books, and supplements available for church musicians gives us a good view of the new and its possibilities for worship renewal. These resources can bring new meaning to ancient stories and symbols; widen our frame of reference, and create the possibility of a deeper piety, a more profound and inclusive unity. How then do we work to integrate the new into our tried-and-true patterns and styles?

Navigating the Rapids of Change

We conclude with some pointers on how to work with conflict and change. The "Aids to Discussion" section of each chapter is a good source for this process. Below are other recommendations.

1. Study your own history. Take a good, long look at who you are. Consider both your links with your tradition, with its grounding in Scripture and history and its particular example as God's faithful witness in your location through the years. Your own history as a congregation could stretch back to the 17th century or to the late decades of the 20th century. Whatever your "age," the founding of your congregation is an important narrative that has shaped your identity ever since.

2. Poll the present congregation. Ask members questions about worship and its meaning for them. Interview them, using parts of the questionnaire in appendix D of this book as a starting point. Tease out their understanding of style. Use the videotape to help you uncover the more hidden meanings of style in your congregation. Style conveys an important core meaning of worship. Help people in the congregation describe it by asking them to talk about worship services that were meaningful to them.

3. Gauge the vitality of your present style. What are your signature symbols? How would you describe your "heart language"? Working within a particular language takes mastery, as we see in the project churches. Note what you are good at.

4. Look to the future. Having looked at the past and the present, shift your focus to the future. Where do you feel the nudge of the "creative event"? Where are the constrictions in your life as a congregation?

5. In all things, seek the creative good, the source of all life. Wieman points out the dangers and pitfalls of the familiar cultural patterns of

a congregation. The "created good" can be used to block the "creative good." It is not necessarily true, however, that change is the creative good in every situation. All styles have limitations, including the new one that seems so shiny in its potential. As one scholar wrote about the changes in worship in the Roman Catholic Church begun in Vatican II: "[Liturgists] demystified our worship, including its cornerstone, the Mass. Something vital, if intangible, was lost with the changes, and thus far apparently no one knows what to do about it."[3] Worship requires repetition. If it changes week by week, a congregation loses a significant path to the depths of its piety. It gets caught up in a surface of kaleidoscopic change, fumbling with unfamiliar words and actions. Remember that there is also the idolatry of the new.

6.   Strike a balance between the old and the new. The wholesale replacement of one style by another is immoral if it succeeds in driving away the part of the congregation that objects to it. Balance and cooperation are the sought-after goals. Whereas the Bible says little about style, it does say quite a lot about the nature of relationships in the community of faith. Plan educational programs and experiments with lots of preparation, giving parishioners opportunities to discuss the proposed changes and their impact on their worship experience. Notice in the "Aids to Discussion" section, people are given the opportunity to talk in groups with people with whom they disagree. Listening to someone talk about the experience of a new style helps the dissenters to understand its power. Conversely, advocates of the new learn from those formed in the old patterns much about the power of worship to sustain people over the long haul.

7.   Know that God works alongside you, confirming you in the narrow path, chiding and correcting you in your folly, nourishing you in your doubts and failures. Wieman speaks to the nature of this God-laden creative event that we serve in this exploration. He says:

The creative event cannot be used to shape the world closer to the heart's desire, because it transforms the heart's desire so that one wants something very different from what one desired in the beginning.[4]

Seeking God rather than what you desired from the beginning keeps the idolatry of both the known and the new at bay. Seeking God requires listening for a transformative word, which often comes when we least expect it. Above all, it requires prayer.

Conclusion: Seeking God Together

In this book, we offer no "cookie-cutter" solutions to style conflicts. Every congregation is different. All congregations are unique communities, made up of people with their complex web of human foibles, well-intentioned motivations, hopes, dreams, pasts, and futures. What we do offer you is an explanation of the way style displays the inner spiritual, communal life of three New England congregations. We say to you, "Here are three stories of style and what it embodies." Then we give you a process to explore your own style and its interrelated piety. Your exploration will lead you in paths we have not yet traveled. We hope that this process of exploration leads you to God, the source of all human good, and to your hoped-for goals in worship renewal. Good luck and Godspeed.

Aids to Discussion

1. Summarize what you have learned by using question #28 in the questionnaire in appendix D, "Worship at Its Best," as the basis for a general discussion.

2. Draw pictures or make collages of your congregation's aspirations for the future. Use them to extend your time line from the past through the present into the future.

3. Describe events of the "creative good" in worship and in other aspects of your lives. Can you think of ways that the "created good" has been a barrier to God in your common worship life?

4. Plan a hymn-sing of new music for worship. Note: This new music may be chronologically "old" but new to your congregation.

5. Outline changes that might be made to your prevailing style. Bring in new worship resources to try out with the group.

Notable Music Resources for Congregations

In this list you will find a selective list of musical resources published within the last five to ten years. We do not claim that any of these resources, particularly the collections, are the best available to you. They are hymnals, alternative collections, supplements, and other resources that may be useful to an average congregation seeking to broaden its worship styles. They are U.S. rather than foreign publications, and multi-authored collections, rather than single-author ones. In this era of extensive worship experimentation and creativity, there is a virtual explosion of resources. We also concentrated on English-language publications, rather than resources completely in other languages. However, many of the publications do contain some texts in other languages.

A resource published by a particular denominational publisher may be useful for any denomination, depending on the orientation or purpose of the resource. Many of these resources have a companion volume, or handbook, that gives background information on contents, performance suggestions, and ideas for integrating the resource into worship. All publishers and many denominations have their own Web sites where information on these and other resources may be found. Also, many of these resources are also available through the Hymn Society of America. The society may be reached by phone 1-800-THE-HYMN and on the Web: www.hymnsociety.org.

DENOMINATIONAL HYMNALS:

The African Methodist Episcopal Zion Bicentennial Hymnal. Bicentennial Hymnal Commission, George W. Walker, Sr., chairman, 1996.

American Baptist Hymnal. Texarkana, Texas: Bogard Press, 1960 (1997
reprint).

Baptist Hymnal. Nashville: Convention Press, Nashville, 1991.

Chalice Hymnal (Christian Church [Disciples of Christ]). Daniel B. Merrick,
ed. St. Louis: Chalice Press, 1995.

Christian Worship: A Lutheran Hymnal (authorized by the Wisconsin
Evangelical Lutheran Synod). Milwaukee: Northwestern Publishing
House, 1993.

The Collegeville Hymnal (Roman Catholic). Edward J. McKenna, ed.
Collegeville, Minn.: Liturgical Press, 1990.

The Covenant Hymnal: A Worshipbook (Evangelical Covenant Church).
Chicago: Covenant Publications, 1996.

Evangelical Lutheran Hymnary (prepared by the Worship Committee of
the Evangelical Lutheran Synod, Mankato, Minn.). St. Louis:
MorningStar Music Publishers, 1996.

Gather (Comprehensive) (Roman Catholic). Chicago: G.I.A. Publications,
1994.

Glory and Praise (2nd edition) (Roman Catholic). Portland: Oregon Catholic
Press (OCP) Publications, 1997.

The Hymnal 1982 (Episcopal). New York: The Church Hymnal Corporation, 1985.

Lead Me, Guide Me: The African American Catholic Hymnal. Chicago:
G.I.A. Publications, 1987.

Lutheran Book of Worship (Evangelical Lutheran Church in America).
Minneapolis: Augsburg Publishing House, 1978.

Lutheran Worship. Prepared by the Commission on Worship of the Lutheran
Church–Missouri Synod. St. Louis: Concordia Publishing House, 1982.

The New Century Hymnal (United Church of Christ). Arthur C. Clyde, ed.
Cleveland: Pilgrim Press, 1995.

The New National Baptist Hymnal. Nashville: National Baptist Publishing
Board, 1977.

The Presbyterian Hymnal: Hymns, Psalms, and Spiritual Songs. LindaJo
McKim, ed. Louisville: Westminster John Knox, 1990.

Psalter Hymnal (Christian Reformed Church). Grand Rapids: CRC Publications, 1988.

RitualSong (Roman Catholic). Chicago: G.I.A. Publications, 1996.

Singing the Living Tradition (Unitarian Universalist). Boston: Unitarian Universalist Association/Beacon Press, 1993.

The United Methodist Hymnal. Carlton R. Young, ed. Nashville: United Methodist Publishing House, 1989.

Worship, 3rd edition. (Roman Catholic). Chicago: G.I.A. Publications, 1986.

COLLECTIONS:

Bring the Feast: Songs from the Re-Imagining Community. Arthur G. Clyde, ed. Cleveland: Pilgrim Press, 1998. A collection of 47 songs, global and ecumenical in perspective, that use new imagery of hope, justice, and healing to integrate the divine feminine. Musical settings are from Latin America, the Asian Rim, and Africa, as well as Europe and America.

Celebrate! Songs for Renewal. Keith Landis, compiler and ed. Whittier, Calif.: Praise Publications, 1998. A comprehensive collection of 234 praise songs, choruses, and service music from several decades, as well as worship songs from many backgrounds. Useful for contemporary worship services, smaller group meetings, and blended worship settings. Topical organization by occasion, season, and function (gathering, entrance, communion), as well as service music; indexes.

The Celebration Hymnal. Tom Fettke, senior ed. Nashville: Word Music/Integrity Music, 1997. Nondenominational, leaning toward evangelical. Designed for use in "blended" worship services. This is a mix of over 800 traditional hymns, contemporary hymns, and praise songs. Numerous indexes.

Come Celebrate! A Hymnal Supplement. Betty Pulkingham, Mimi Farra, and Kevin Hackett, eds. Pacific, Mo.:Mel Bay Publications, 1990. (Supplements *The Hymnal 1982* [Episcopal].) New texts and music for the daily office, Eucharist, canticles, and seasonal and topical hymns. Contents are eclectic, with international and intergenerational emphases. Performance notes, indexes.

The Courage to Say No: Twenty-three Songs for Lent and Easter. John L. Bell and Graham Maule, eds. Iona Community/Wild Goose Resource Group (Chicago: G.I.A. Publications, North American publisher and distributor), 1996. Seasonal English texts, incorporating songs from

African and African American traditions. The four-part harmony of
many songs facilitates their use as choral arrangements.

The Faith We Sing. Nashville: Abingdon, 2000. (Newest supplement to
The United Methodist Hymnal.) Includes newer contemporary/praise
music and hymns; world music (Africa, Europe, Asia), African American and Hispanic American music; and modern Taizé chants.

For the Living of These Days: Resources for Enriching Worship. C.
Michael Hawn, ed. Macon, Ga.: Smyth & Helwys, Publishing, 1995.
Includes hymns that reflect the diversity of thought within the free-
church (Baptist) tradition. The texts address contemporary issues and
are drawn from various ethnic traditions. Biographies of contributors,
indexes.

Global Praise 1. S. T. Kimbrough, Jr., and Carlton R. Young, eds. New
York: General Board of Global Ministries, United Methodist Church,
GBGMusik, 1996 (and subsequent revisions through 1999). Traditional
and contemporary texts and music from around the world. This ecumenical resource includes songs from diverse cultures and languages
(transliterations for Chinese, Korean, and Russian texts are provided),
set to simple music. The Companion Program and Resource Book
provides introductory articles, programs, workshops, worship resources,
and liturgies.

Global Praise 2. Songs for Worship and Witness. S. T. Kimbrough, Jr.,
and Carlton R. Young, eds. New York: General Board of Global Ministries, United Methodist Church, GBGMusik, 2000. A second ecumenical collection of 122 songs and service music from around the world,
arranged topically. Localities represented include Asia, Africa, the
Caribbean, Europe, North and South American, and the islands of the
Pacific.

*Global Songs 2: Songs of Faith, Hope, and Liberation from the Church
Around the World*. Minneapolis: Augsburg Fortress, 1997. Includes
songs from Africa, Latin America and the Caribbean, North America,
Europe, and Asia. All non-English texts have an English translation or
paraphrase. Background notes include performance suggestions. Indexes.

*Halle, Halle: We Sing the World Round. Songs from the World Church
for Children, Youth, and Congregation*. C. Michael Hawn, compiler
and author. Garland, Texas: Choristers Guild, 1999. A multicultural
songbook containing 36 songs from Africa, Latin America, and Asia,

grouped by function, season, or topic. English translations or paraphrases are provided. The director's edition includes ideas for teaching the music and notes on instrumentation and performance practices.

Hymnal Supplement 98. St. Louis: Concordia Publishing House, 1998. Simplified forms of congregational services. A wide span of musical styles from many communities is represented, including hymnody of Africa, China, and Latin America. Texts span early Christianity through the 20th century. Orders of service and indexes.

Hymns from the Four Winds. Nashville: Abingdon, 1983. A collection of 125 Asian and Asian-American hymns in English, many newly written or recently adapted. The emphasis is on distinctly Asian traditions. Notes and performance suggestions.

Lift Every Voice and Sing II: An African American Hymnal. New York: Church Publishing Incorporated, 1993. (Supplements *The Hymnal 1982* [Episcopal].) Spirituals, traditional and contemporary gospel songs, missionary and evangelistic hymns. Service music and mass settings in traditional and gospel settings. Performance notes.

Lift Up Your Hearts: Songs for Creative Worship. Linda White, ed. Louisville: Geneva Press, 2000. A supplement for *The Presbyterian Hymnal,* but useful in other settings. More than 140 hymns and songs to introduce contemporary music into worship. Songs of praise, thanksgiving, mission, prayer; service music. The worship leader's edition provides planning ideas.

Lord Be Glorified: A New Hymnal Supplement for Blended Worship. Larry Pugh, ed. Dayton, Ohio: Lorenz Publishing, 1999. A general supplement designed to complement denominational hymnals. Contemporary music and texts, including praise choruses, reflect the growing diversity of styles and functions in worship.

Many and Great: Songs of the World Church (vol. 1). (See also vol. 2, *Sent by the Lord.*) John L. Bell, ed. and arr. Chicago: G.I.A. Publications, 1990. Songs for devotion and worship from around the world, all with an English translation or paraphrase. Brief notes accompany each selection.

New Century Psalter. Burton H. Throckmorton Jr., and Arthur G. Clyde, eds. Cleveland: Pilgrim Press, 1999. All 150 Psalms, using inclusive language. Includes a lectionary, orders for morning and evening prayer, and directions for singing the psalms and antiphons.

New Songs of Rejoicing. David P. Schaap, ed. Kingston, N.Y.: Selah Publishing, 1994. An anthology of 171 hymns and psalm settings whose words or music (or both) have not previously appeared in a mainstream hymnal. Texts are for all seasons and occasions of worship. Extensive indexes.

Renew! Songs and Hymns for Blended Worship. Robert Webber, Vicky Tusken, John Witvliet, and Jack Schrader, eds. Carol Stream, Ill.: Hope Publishing, 1995. Traditional and contemporary worship songs for use in blended worship. Organization follows the four-fold pattern of worship: gathering, hearing God's Word, giving thanks, and sending forth. Includes songs and settings for communion.

Sent by the Lord: Songs of the World Church (vol. 2). (See also vol. 1, *Many and Great.*) John L. Bell, ed. and arr. Chicago: G.I.A. Publications, 1990. Songs for devotion and worship from around the world, all with an English translation or paraphrase. Brief notes accompany each selection.

Sing Justice! Do Justice! A Collection of New Hymns and Songs with New and Familiar Tunes. Kingston, N.Y.: Selah Publishing, 1998. Hymns on issues of justice and stewardship in the world. The 25 texts, the result of an international search, are set to familiar tunes as well as to new music.

Sing to Our God New Songs of Rejoicing. David P. Schaap, ed. Kingstown, N.Y.: Selah Publishing, 2000. Selah's third hymnal supplement. Includes 157 hymns, many in print for the first time, organized by the church year and general topics. Includes psalms and canticle settings.

Songs for a Gospel People. R. Gerald Hobbs, ed. Winfield, British Columbia: Wood Lake Books, 1991. Hymnal supplement that reflects a worldwide ecumenical heritage. Includes 134 traditional and new hymns. Minimal indexes.

Songs for Life. Grand Rapids: CRC Publications, 1994. A hymnal especially for preschool through sixth grade that focuses on the "gathering time" in church education programs. Includes more than 250 songs from around the world, some in other languages. Styles include historic hymns, new psalm settings, Scripture choruses, and call-and-response songs. There is also an excellent leader's guide with extensive notes.

Songs of Zion. Nashville: Abingdon, 1981. Hymns, gospel songs, spirituals, and liturgical music from the African American heritage and tradition as well as contemporary experience. The introduction includes performance practice notes and a short essay on the hymn in the black worship experience.

Spirit Anew: Singing Prayer & Praise. Alan C. Whitmore, ed. Kelowna, British Columbia: Wood Lake Books, Inc., 1999. Over 175 contemporary, inclusive-language hymns in a variety of styles, including mantras, African American spirituals, seasonal songs, and music from other cultures. The texts are "less wordy and easier to sing than standard worship music."

Supplement 99. George H. Shorney, ed. Carol Stream, Ill.: Hope Publishing, 1999. The sixth in a series of hymnal supplements that makes available new works of contemporary authors and composers. In addition to the "standard" topics, there are texts on subjects such as art and artists, disasters, ecology, and world peace. A topical index; pictures and short biographies of the authors and composers.

This Far by Faith. Minneapolis: Augsburg Fortress, 1999. (Supplements Lutheran worship books.) An African American resource of over 300 hymns, songs, and liturgical settings: spirituals, traditional and contemporary gospel, choruses, and familiar standards. Includes jazz and blues, and music from Africa and the Caribbean. Extensive indexes.

Voices: Native American Hymns and Worship Resources. The Native American Hymnal and Worship Resources Committee. Nashville: Discipleship Resources, 1992. Hymns and worship resources from a variety of Native American groups. Original languages and English translations or paraphrases, and a guide to pronunciation.

With One Voice (enlarged edition). Minneapolis: Augsburg Fortress, 1996. (Supplement to the *Lutheran Book of Worship*.) New liturgical settings, hymns, and songs from North American cultures as well as from around the world. Some choruses and Taizé music; use of inclusive language, alternative images of God.

Wonder, Love, and Praise. William Wunsch, ed. New York: Church Publishing, Inc., 1997. (Supplements *The Hymnal 1982* [Episcopal].) Seasonal and topical hymns and songs in a variety of musical styles from many cultures. New settings of service music and canticles; inclusive language; some texts in languages other than English. The companion *Leader's Guide* (John L. Hooker, ed.) is especially helpful.

Worship and Praise Songbook. Minneapolis: Augsburg Fortress, 1999. (A companion to the Lutheran Book of Worship [ELCA].) More than 150 contemporary songs and choruses in blended musical styles, including music for the Eucharist, baptism, and daily prayer; Psalm and Scripture songs; and seasonal tunes.

Select Bibliography

Ammerman, Nancy, Jackson W. Carroll, and Carl S. Dudley. *Studying Congregations*. Nashville: Abingdon Press, 1998.

Barron, Hall. *Those Who Stayed Behind: Rural Society in Nineteenth-Century New England*. Cambridge [Cambridgeshire] and New York: Cambridge University Press, 1984.

Bellah, Robert N., et al. *Habits of the Heart*. Berkeley: University of California Press, 1985.

Choy, Bong-yeon. *Koreans in America*. Chicago: Nelson-Hall Press, 1979.

Clark, Linda J. *Music in Churches*. Bethesda: Alban Institute, 1995.

————. "Hymn-singing: Aesthetic Forms as Carriers of Religious Tradition." Carl Dudley et al., *Carriers of Faith*. Louisville: Westminster John Knox, 1991.

Colaw, Emerson. *Beliefs of a United Methodist Christian*. Nashville: Discipleship Resources, 1987.

Danto, Arthur C. *Beyond the Brillo Box: The Visual Arts in Post-Historical Perspective*. New York: Noonday Press, 1992.

————. *The Transfiguration of the Commonplace*. Cambridge: Harvard University Press, 1981.

DuBois, W. E. B. *Dusk of Dawn*. New Introduction by Herbert Aptheker. Millwood, N.Y.: Kraus-Thomson Org. Limited, 1975 (reprint of 1940 ed.).

Dulles, Avery, S.J. *Models of the Church*. Garden City, N.Y.: Doubleday, 1974.

Dykstra, Craig. "Reconceiving Practice." Barbara Wheeler and Edward Farley, eds. *Shifting Boundaries*. Louisville: Westminster John Knox, 1991.

Edwards, Rheable M., and Laura Norris. "The Negro in Boston." ABCD
    (Action for Boston Community Development), Nov. 1961 [unpublished
    ms.].
Ferris, William R., Jr. "The Negro Conversion," *Keystone Folklore Quar-
    terly* 26 (Sept. 1970): 35f.
Geertz, Clifford. "Art as a Cultural System" *Modern Language Notes
    (MLN)* 91 (1976): 1473f.
———. "Ethos, World View, and the Analysis of Sacred Symbols." *The
    Interpretation of Symbols.* New York: Basic Books, 1973.
George, Carol V. *Segregated Sabbath: Richard Allen and the Emer-
    gence of Independent Black Churches 1760-1840.* New York:
    Oxford University Press, 1973.
Hanson, Paul D. *The People Called: The Growth of Community.* San
    Francisco: Harper & Row, 1986.
Hayden, Robert C. *Faith, Culture and Leadership: A History of the
    Black Church in Boston.* Boston: Boston Public Library, 1983.
Higginson, Thomas Wentworth. "Negro Spirituals." *Atlantic Monthly* 19
    (June 1867): 685f.
Hochschild, Arlie. *The Managed Heart: Commercialization of Human
    Feeling.* Berkeley: University of California Press, 1983.
Holifield, E. Brooks. *The Covenant Sealed: The Development of Puritan
    Sacramental Theology in Old and New England, 1570-1720.* New
    Haven: Yale University Press, 1974.
Hoon, Paul W. *The Integrity of Worship.* Nashville: Abingdon, 1971.
Hurh, Won Moo. "The Korean-American Community: Its Development in
    Historical and Comparative Perspectives." *Modern Praxis* 9 (fall 1989):
    245f.
Hurh, Won Moo, and Kwang Chung Kim. *Korean Immigrants in America:
    A Structural Analysis of Ethnic Confinement and Adhesive Adap-
    tation.* Rutherford, N.J.: Associated University Presses, 1984.
Jennings, Theodore. *The Liturgy of Liberation.* Nashville: Abingdon, 1988.
Jones, Lawrence. "They Sought a City: The Black Church and Churchmen
    in the 19th Century." *USQR* 26 (1971): 253f.
Kim, Illsoo. "Organizational Patterns of Korean American Methodists
    Churches: Denominationalism and Personal Communities." *Rethink-
    ing Methodist History*, R. E. Richey and K. E. Rowe, eds. Nashville:
    Kingswood Books, 1985.
Langer, Susanne K. *Philosophy in a New Key*, 3rd ed. Cambridge: Harvard
    University Press, 1942.

Levine, Lawrence. *Black Culture and Black Consciousness: Afro-American Folk Thought from Slavery to Freedom.* New York: Oxford University Press, 1977.

_____. *The Unpredictable Past.* New York: Oxford University Press, 1993.

Lincoln, C. Eric, and Lawrence Mamiya. *The Black Church in the African-American Experience.* Durham, N.C.: Duke University, 1990.

Mangiafico, Luciano. *Contemporary American Immigrants: Patterns of Filipino, Korean, and Chinese Settlement in the U. S.* New York: Praeger, 1988.

Mathews, Donald G. "The Second Great Awakening as an Organizing Principle." *American Quarterly* 21, 23f

McDannel, Colleen. *Material Christianity.* New Haven: Yale University Press, 1995.

Meland, Bernard E. "Myth as a Mode of Awareness and Intelligibility." *American Journal of Theology and Philosophy* 8 (1987): 109f.

Messer, Donald. *Images of Christian Ministry.* Nashville: Abingdon, 1989.

Meyrowitz, Joshua. *No Sense of Place: The Impact of Electronic Media on Social Behavior.* New York: Oxford University Press, 1985.

Miller, Perry. *The New England Mind from Colony to Province.* Cambridge: Harvard University Press, 1953.

Moberg, David O. *The Church as a Social Institution.* Grand Rapids: Baker Book House, 1962.

Pope, Robert G. *The Half-Way Covenant: Church Membership in Puritan New England.* Princeton: Princeton University Press, 1969.

Power, David N., *Unsearchable Riches: The Symbolic Nature of Liturgy.* New York: Pueblo, 1984.

Roof, W. Clark, and William McKinney. *American Mainline Religion.* New Brunswick: Rutgers University Press, 1987.

Roozen, David A., William McKinney, and Jackson W. Carroll. *Varieties of Religious Presence.* New York: Pilgrim Press, 1984.

Ross, Alex. "The Musical Kaleidoscope." *New Yorker* (Aug. 26–Sept. 2, 1996): 9f.

Schaller, Joseph J. "Performative Language Theory: An Exercise in the Analysis of Ritual." *Worship* 62, #5 (Sept. 1988): 415f.

Searle, Mark. "New Tasks, New Methods: The Emergence of Pastoral Liturgical Studies." *Worship* 57 (July 1983): 291f.

Smith, Timothy. "Slavery and Theology." *Church History* 41 (1972): 497f.

Southern, Eileen. "Musical Practices in Black Churches of Philadelphia and New York, ca 1800-1844." *Journal of the American Musicological Society* 30 (summer 1977): 302f.

Stout, Harry S. *The New England Soul: Preaching and Religious Culture in Colonial New England.* New York: Oxford University Press, 1986.

Thompson, Bard. *Liturgies of the Western Church.* New York: World Publishing, 1961.

Turkle, Sherry. *Life on the Screen.* New York: Simon & Schuster, 1995.

Van Eck, Caroline, James McCallister, and Renee van de Vall, eds. *The Question of Style in Philosophy and the Arts.* Cambridge, England: Cambridge University Press, 1995.

Walden, Daniel. "The Contemporary Opposition to the Political and Educational Ideas of Booker T. Washington." *Journal of Negro History* 45 (1960): 105f.

Walker, Williston. *The Creeds and Platforms of Congregationalism.* New York: Pilgrim Press, 1991.

Walton, Janet. *Art and Worship.* New York: M. Glazier, 1988

Wang, Zhang Sen. *History of Chinese Protestant Church in Boston.* CMI Publishing House, 1997.

Westermeyer, Paul. *Te Deum: The Church and Music.* Minneapolis: Fortress Press, 1998.

White, James F. *Documents of Christian Worship.* Louisville: Westminster John Knox, 1992.

———. *Introduction to Christian Worship.* 2nd ed. Nashville: Abingdon, 1991.

Wieman, Henry N. *The Source of Human Good.* Atlanta: Scholars Press, 1995.

Williams-Jones, Pearl. "Afro-American Gospel Music: A Crystallization of the Black Aesthetic." *Ethnomusicology* 19 (1975): 373f.

Willimon, William H. *Why I Am a United Methodist.* Nashville: Discipleship Resources, 1987.

Wuthnow, Robert. *The Restructuring of American Religion: Society and Faith since World War II.* Princeton: Princeton University Press, 1988.

———. *The Struggle for America's Soul: Evangelicals, Liberals, and Secularism.* Grand Rapids: Eerdmans, 1989.

Project Design

Research Question: What role does style play in the corporate religious identity of this congregation?

Step 1: Team members, as participant/observers, are resident in the congregation from Palm Sunday of one year to Easter of the second year, attending worship and other activities, keeping field notes, and doing interviews. Worship bulletins for the present year and the last five years are collected. Demographic information about the town and its history are collected and studied.

Step 2: Services at the church are videotaped. These are then viewed and analyzed by participant/observers and project director. Questions for analysis: What are the symbols and rituals observed, and how are they displayed? What is the style of the assembly and of its music?

Videotaping: Prior to the taping, film director will go to each church to observe worship. He will then meet with researchers to design the shoot. The research team will provide him a checklist of important elements of worship, drawn up by resident researcher and tested out with specific people in the congregation.

Step 3: Team returns to the church and shows an edited version of the videotape, consisting of worship in the "home" church and intercuts of the other two. Afterward the congregation breaks up into focus groups (by populations such as cradle/switcher,[1] old-timers, newcomers, choir, elected leaders like delegates to annual conference, staff, groups in the center of the church and those on the periphery). These groups will be led by researchers who, through questioning, will provoke a discussion on the following topics: "What is important to understand about the faith of your congregation, and how do worship and its symbols display it?" "How does style communicate what is important?" The researchers' purpose is to stimulate an interpretation of what happens in worship and a reaction to the different styles of worship displayed by the other congregations. These interviews are recorded and transcribed, but not videotaped.

Step 4: A questionnaire is sent out to the parish rolls.

Step 5: A series of exit interviews are conducted with target people, including formal and reputational leaders of the congregation, starting with questions about the corporate and moving to the individual in relationship to the corporate. Possible questions:

1. Can you describe the kinds of people who gather here?
2. Are you like them? In what way?
3. Do they believe the same things you do?
4. What is distinctive about the way your congregation worships? Could you give some examples? (Questions about the various aspects that have been unearthed in the preceding work.)
5. What would you miss if you had to leave?
6. Tell a story that would characterize this church at its best and at its worst.
7. How is the church different from other organizations to which you belong?
8. I am going to ask you to use your imagination on this question. Close your eyes and picture yourself walking or driving down the street where the church is located, on your way somewhere. If you happened to look over at it, what would you think of first?
9. How would the people in your town or neighborhood describe this church? Is it an accurate description?
10. The word "Methodist" appears in the name of your church. What does that mean to you?

11. What are your favorite hymns, choruses, songs, responses? Choose one to tell why it is your favorite. Are there personal memories attached to it? Events in the life of this or any other congregation?
12. Do you think this congregation has a favorite hymn? What is it? Why do you think that hymn is its favorite?

Step 6: The staff is interviewed. Questions asked of the pastor(s), musician(s), and other members of the staff could be more direct, including questions about the identity of this congregation and its sources. Direct questions about style and musical vocabulary could also be asked of the musicians.

Step 7: Organization and analysis of data.

1. An analysis and listing of the "texts" produced in step 3 to uncover important symbols and acts and their meaning.
2. An analysis and listing of hymn repertoires of the congregations and the music mentioned in step 5, question 10 for dominant images/concepts of God, Jesus, the church, the singer.
3. A description of the style of the congregations' assemblies.
4. A comparison of the emerging picture of the congregation with its history and history of town/region.
5. Creation of a "theological map" as embedded in worship and music and in the answers to questions in interviews.
6. Creation of a "cultural map" as embedded in the material of the project.

Step 8: Return to congregation to check out conclusions.

The Congregational Questionnaire

GREETINGS:

For the last several years, the School of Theology at Boston University has been involved in a series of studies of music in worship in churches in the area. Its purpose is to gather information about music and the worship of the community that gathers on a Sunday. It is hoped that the information gathered through this study will illuminate the ways that music can and does support the worship of the congregation and how worship functions to build up the faith lives of the people of the church.

The first study engaged 24 churches in Southern New England. It entailed an in-depth look at one Sunday in many churches. The current study, in which your congregation is involved, concentrates on three congregations over a period of one year. A member of the research team has been coming to church for the last several months. In the fall of 1993, a worship service was videotaped. In the current phase of the project, interviewing is taking place.

This questionnaire provides information about you and your congregation that will help complete the picture of your church's worship, its music, and its faith. Most of the questions in the booklet are easy to answer. We realize, however, that some of the questions may not be so easy; they will require that you think about things you may not often consider. Allow yourself time to think. Please understand that the purpose of this questionnaire is not to judge whether your views are "right" or "wrong" but simply to collect them.

We also want to assure you that the anonymity of your answers is guaranteed. Neither your pastor nor anyone else in your congregation will ever see your answers. All results will be presented as percentages in tables.

The surveys are identified for purposes of keeping track of the process of filling them out. When they are collated, the name will be separated from each questionnaire.

When you have filled out all of the questionnaire with answers that reflect your feelings, please seal it in the envelope provided, and either mail it back to us or give it to your class leader.

We thank you in advance for your time and your cooperation. Your ideas and viewpoints will be of great use to the local churches, to the School of Theology, and to the wider church.

Instructions

Please answer all questions in the order in which they appear in this booklet. Questions have been arranged to make it easy for you to go from one to another. Please read each question carefully.

For most of the questions you will circle *one answer only*. In some questions, however, you are asked to CIRCLE ALL THOSE THAT APPLY OR RANK IN ORDER OF PRIORITY. Here is an example:

(20) What part of the music in worship is the most meaningful to you? (INDICATE YOUR PREFERENCES IN ORDER BY NUMBERING THREE OF THE FOLLOWING LIST 1ST, 2ND, 3RD.)

_____ 1. Hymns and other congregational songs
_____ 2. Anthems and special selections by the choir and/or soloists
_____ 3. Psalm responses
_____ 4. Organ prelude
_____ 5. Organ postlude
_____ 6. Liturgical responses like the Doxology or Gloria Patri
_____ 7. Instrumental music
_____ 8. Other _____

Also, some questions ask you to write your ideas in your own words or to complete pictures that are partly provided. If you read all directions carefully, you will probably not have many problems.

Finally, please make sure you answer *every* question that applies to you. If none of the answers provided for a question seems to fit your thinking perfectly, choose the answer that comes closest. Also, don't ask someone else in your household to fill out part of the questionnaire.

Part I

The questions in this section are addressed to you as a member of a church community; why you come to church and what you do here. Your answers help us to understand the community that worships on Sunday.

(1) Put the time of the service of worship that you usually attend:

_____

(2) In what year did you start attending this church? _____

(3) With so many competing demands placed on our time, it's often difficult to get involved in many activities, committees, auxiliaries, or ministries in a church.

1. Last month, how many hours did you spend doing church work? (Please do not include the hours spent at worship.)

_____

_____

2. Was last month typical of your involvement?

_____

_____

If not, how many hours do you *typically* spend?

_____

_____

3. List the activities that you participated in last month.

_____

_____

_____

_____

(4) Think of five people who are your closest friends. (Do not include relatives.) How many of these friends are also members of your church? (CIRCLE ONE)

$$0 \qquad 1 \qquad 2 \qquad 3 \qquad 4 \qquad 5$$

(5) In general, how well does this parish meet: (CIRCLE ONE NUMBER BESIDE EACH STATEMENT)

	completely	very well	not very well	not at all
Your spiritual needs	1	2	3	4
Your social needs	1	2	3	4

(6) People go to church for different reasons. From the list below, please circle only the most important reason you attend worship at your church. (CIRCLE ONE)

1. Mainly, it's a habit.
2. I want to please or satisfy someone close to me (e.g., spouse or parent).
3. I want to provide values for my children.
4. I enjoy being with other people in our church.
5. I enjoy taking part in the service itself.
6. I enjoy the feeling of meditating and communicating with God.
7. I feel a need to hear God's word.
8. I feel a need to receive the sacrament of Holy Communion.
9. I feel a need for insight and guidance.
10. Other (INDICATE REASON IN THE SPACE)

_____

(7) How many of your family members attend this church? (CIRCLE ONE)

$$0 \qquad 1 \qquad 2 \qquad 3 \qquad 4 \qquad 5 \qquad \text{6 or more}$$

(8) How would you assess the importance of worship in this church to your ongoing faith? (CIRCLE ONLY ONE)

1. Very important
2. Important
3. Not very important
4. Of no importance

(9) The following statements reflect various activities of the church. For each item would you indicate whether this activity is very important, somewhat important, not very important or contradictory to YOUR UNDERSTANDING OF THE CHURCH'S MISSION in today's world.

Key to Answers
1= CT =contradictory to
2= NI =Not very important
3= SI =Somewhat important
4= VI =Very important

HOW IMPORTANT
for Mission of Church today?

		CT	NI	SI	VI
1.	Providing adult education resources that bring laity face to face with urban and rural problems, racial discrimination, world poverty and hunger, and other social issues.	1	2	3	4
2.	Establishing new churches.	1	2	3	4
3.	Helping church members resist the temptation to experiment with new lifestyles.	1	2	3	4
4.	Actively reaching out to members of other religious groups with an invitation to find true salvation.	1	2	3	4

		CT	NI	SI	VI
5.	Encouraging pastors of local churches to speak out in public on social, political, and economic issues that confront American society today.	1	2	3	4
6.	Opening members' hearts and minds to the spiritual gifts of miracles, and healing, and to the baptism of the Holy Spirit.	1	2	3	4
7.	Encouraging church members to reach their own decisions on issues of faith and morals even if this diminishes the church's ability to speak with a single voice on these issues.	1	2	3	4
8.	Promoting social justice in North America and throughout the world by the use of organized, collective action.	1	2	3	4
9.	Reminding Christians of their duty to uphold and defend their country and the values it stands for.	1	2	3	4
10.	Protecting church members from the false teachings of other religious groups.	1	2	3	4
11.	Encouraging church members to adhere faithfully to civil laws, even when they disagree with them.	1	2	3	4
12.	Listening carefully to what the world is saying in order to understand what the church's ministry should be about.	1	2	3	4
13.	Encouraging church members to make explicit declarations of their personal faith to friends, neighbors, and co-workers.	1	2	3	4

	CT	NI	SI	VI
14. Making the church a place where people of all classes and races are included.	1	2	3	4
15. Encouraging and inspiring church members, as individuals, to become involved in social and political issues.	1	2	3	4
16. Finding ways to involve women and people of color in decision-making roles within the church.	1	2	3	4
17. Supporting evangelical missions overseas to convert the world to Christ.	1	2	3	4
18. Providing relief and physical support to people and groups in need in this country and around the world.	1	2	3	4
19. Maintaining an appropriate distance between the churches and governmental affairs.	1	2	3	4
20. Preparing church members for a world to come in which the cares of this world are absent.	1	2	3	4
21. Encouraging members to develop their spiritual life through prayer and Bible study.	1	2	3	4

Part II

This next set of questions concerns your musical interests and talents. It helps us gain information about a congregation's view of music in worship and worshipers' participation in it.

(10) Do you consider yourself a musician?   1. Yes   2. No

(11) Circle the church musical organizations or activities in which you have participated in the last five years.

    1. Adult choir
    2. Children's choir
    3. Young adults' choir
    4. Handbells
    5. Instrumental groups
    6. Music committee
    7. Other:

    _____

(12) Do you read music?   1. Yes   2. No

(13) Do you play a musical instrument?   1. Yes   2. No

(14) Do you participate in musical organizations in the community (e.g. choral societies, instrumental ensembles, barber shop quartets, jazz bands)?

                                         1. Yes   2. No

(15) In the last six months have you participated in formal or informal group singing anywhere except in church?

                                         1. Yes   2. No

(16) How often do you listen to music on the radio?

    Number of hours a week: _____

    Type of music: _____

                            _____

(17) How often do you attend public concerts?

    1. Once a year
    2. Twice a year
    3. Once a month or more

(18) The world is filled with all kinds of music. Arrange the following list of "musics" in order of your preference by numbering them 1-12.

    ___ 01 Folk music
    ___ 02 Rock 'n' roll
    ___ 03 Jazz and the blues
    ___ 04 Classical/symphonic
    ___ 05 Opera
    ___ 06 Musicals
    ___ 07 Sacred music (anthems, oratorios, organ music, etc.)
    ___ 08 Gospel music
    ___ 09 Chamber music
    ___ 10 Contemporary Christian
    ___ 11 Country and western
    ___ 12 Other:

_____

(19) If you could make one change in the present music program to make it more effective, what would it be?

_____

(20) What part of the music in worship is the most meaningful to you? (INDICATE YOUR PREFERENCES IN ORDER BY NUMBERING THREE OF THE FOLLOWING LIST 1ST, 2ND, 3RD.)

    ___ 1. Hymns and other congregational songs
    ___ 2. Anthems and special selections by the choir and/or soloists
    ___ 3. Psalm responses
    ___ 4. Organ prelude
    ___ 5. Organ postlude
    ___ 6. Liturgical responses like the Doxology or Gloria Patri
    ___ 7. Instrumental music
    ___ 8. Other:

_____

(21) How would you rank yourself as a singer? (CIRCLE ONE)

    1. I don't like to sing.
    2. I like to sing but don't do it well.
    3. I like to sing and do it well.
    4. I do not like to sing but enjoy standing and listening to others.

(22) Which of the following statements comes closest to your view of the kind of music to be used in worship? (CIRCLE ONE)

    1. All styles of music are appropriate to worship.
    2. Any music is appropriate so long as it is sung or played with sincerity.
    3. Any kind of music is appropriate as long as I find it enjoyable.
    4. Since music in worship is an offering to God, only the best kind is appropriate.
    5. Any kind of music is appropriate as long as the congregation can use it to praise God.
    6. Any kind of music is appropriate provided that it is done well.
    7. Other:

_____

_____

(23) Hymns often teach us very powerful lessons about God and God's relationship to us. Think of your favorite hymn. (IF YOU HAVE SEVERAL, PLEASE CHOOSE THE ONE THAT FIRST CAME TO MIND.)

    1. What is your favorite hymn?

_____

    2. Why is this hymn your favorite?

_____

_____

Part III

Here the questions are addressed to you as a person of faith. They provide an opportunity for you to describe what your religious faith really means to you.

(24) How often do you go to each of the following? (CIRCLE ONLY ONE NUMBER BESIDE EACH)

		Daily	Several times a week	Once a week	2 or 3 times a month	Once a month	Several times a year	Once a year or less	Never
1.	Sunday morning services			3	4	5	6	7	8
2.	Sunday evening services			3	4	5	6	7	8
3.	Sunday school	1	2	3	4	5	6	7	8
4.	Midweek services	1	2	3	4	5	6	7	8
5.	Prayer meetings	1	2	3	4	5	6	7	8
6.	Other (please list)	1	2	3	4	5	6	7	8

_____

(25) How often do you do the following: (CIRCLE ONE NUMBER FOR EACH)

1.	Read or study the Bible on your own	1	2	3	4	5	6	7	8
2.	Read or study the Bible with Bible with friends or as part of a group	1	2	3	4	5	6	7	8
3.	Say grace before meals	1	2	3	4	5	6	7	8
4.	Share your religious beliefs with others who have *similar* beliefs	1	2	3	4	5	6	7	8
5.	Share your religious beliefs with those who have *different* beliefs	1	2	3	4	5	6	7	8
6.	Listen to a religious program on radio (SPECIFY WHICH PROGRAMS)	1	2	3	4	5	6	7	8

7.	Watch a religious program on TV (SPECIFY WHICH PROGRAMS)	1	2	3	4	5	6	7	8
8.	Pray with members of family or friends other than table grace	1	2	3	4	5	6	7	8
9.	Pray privately	1	2	3	4	5	6	7	8
10.	Go on retreats or other religious weekends or gatherings	1	2	3	4	5	6	7	8
11.	Go to revivals or other religious services in other churches	1	2	3	4	5	6	7	8

(26) Below is a list of images that could be used to describe God. INDICATE HOW ACCURATE YOU FEEL EACH IMAGE IS AS A DESCRIPTION OF GOD.

	Completely Inaccurate				Completely Accurate
1. Judge	1	2	3	4	5
2. Protector	1	2	3	4	5
3. Redeemer	1	2	3	4	5
4. Lover	1	2	3	4	5
5. Master	1	2	3	4	5
6. Mother	1	2	3	4	5
7. Creator	1	2	3	4	5
8. Father	1	2	3	4	5
9. Friend	1	2	3	4	5

(27) As you read each of the following phrases, indicate how true it is for you. (CIRCLE ONLY ONE NUMBER BESIDE EACH STATEMENT OR PHRASE)

	Not true at all				Extremely true
God is:					
1. Faithful	1	2	3	4	5
2. Dependable	1	2	3	4	5
3. Forgiving	1	2	3	4	5
4. Mysterious	1	2	3	4	5
5. More present in relationships with others than in an individual's life	1	2	3	4	5
6. Distant	1	2	3	4	5
7. Permissive	1	2	3	4	5
8. A creative force in history	1	2	3	4	5
9. Aware of everything I think	1	2	3	4	5
10. Close	1	2	3	4	5
11. Vindictive	1	2	3	4	5
12. My constant companion	1	2	3	4	5
13. Strict	1	2	3	4	5
14. Clearly knowable	1	2	3	4	5
15. In my life more as a symbol or an idea than as a real presence I can feel	1	2	3	4	5
16. All-powerful	1	2	3	4	5
17. Awesome	1	2	3	4	5
18. Fascinating	1	2	3	4	5
19. Judgmental	1	2	3	4	5
20. Indifferent	1	2	3	4	5

(28) Below are six drawings of people at worship. Circle the one that most clearly captures your view of worship at its best. There is a space included for you to add one of your own if the others are inadequate.

(29) The following questions deal with your feelings of "closeness" to God in different situations. (PLEASE CIRCLE ONLY ONE NUMBER FOR EACH STATEMENT. OMIT THOSE WHICH ARE NOT APPLICABLE TO YOUR EXPERIENCE.)

	Not close at all		Somewhat close		Very close
How close to God do you feel while:					
1. Reading the Bible	1	2	3	4	5
2. Gathering with members of the congregation at fellowship events	1	2	3	4	5
3. Attending worship	1	2	3	4	5
4. Singing in church	1	2	3	4	5
5. Receiving Holy Communion	1	2	3	4	5
6. Praying privately	1	2	3	4	5
7. Helping individuals in need	1	2	3	4	5
8. Working for the church	1	2	3	4	5
9. Working for justice and peace	1	2	3	4	5
10. Being out in nature	1	2	3	4	5
11. Being with the person I love	1	2	3	4	5
12. Going on retreats	1	2	3	4	5
13. Meeting with a small church group for prayer and support	1	2	3	4	5
14. Obeying the Ten Commandments	1	2	3	4	5

(30) How often in your life have you had an experience when you felt as though you were very close to a powerful, spiritual force that seemed to lift you out of yourself? (CIRCLE ONE)

1. Never in my life (SKIP THE NEXT QUESTION)
2. Once or twice
3. Several times
4. Often

(31) When you have or had these religious experiences, what happened?
(e.g., When did it happen? How did it happen? How did you feel?
Why did you think it was a spiritual force?) PLEASE DESCRIBE.

_____

_____

_____

_____

_____

_____

_____

_____

_____

_____

_____

_____

_____

_____

Part IV

It is important for us to know not only why you come to worship on Sunday morning but also who you are. Please answer the following questions about yourself.

(32) Sex (CIRCLE ONE)   1. Male   2. Female

(33) What is your present marital status? (CIRCLE ONE)

    1. Never married
    2. Married and living with spouse
    3. Separated
    4. Divorced and now single
    5. Divorced and now remarried
    6. Widow or widower
    7. Other: _____

(34) Do you have any children? If so, how many and what are their ages?

    1. I have no children.
    2. I have one child.
    3. I have _____ children.

    (a) List the ages of the youngest and the oldest below.

        Youngest: _____
        Oldest: _____

(35) Besides being an American, what is your main national origin? (CIRCLE THOSE THAT APPLY)

    01 American (no other nationality)
    02 African-American
    03 English
    04 Welsh, Scots
    05 French-speaking Canadian
    06 French
    07 Eastern European
    08 Italian   *(list continues)*

09 Portuguese
10 Asian (Korean, Chinese, Japanese, Vietnamese, etc.)
11 Middle Eastern (Arab, Lebanese, Syrian, Egyptian, etc.)
12 Amer-Indian (Native American)
13 German
14 Latino
15 English-speaking Canadian
16 Scandinavian
17 Irish
18 West Indian
19 Other:

---

(36) Please indicate the highest level of education you have completed.
(CIRCLE ONLY ONE)

1. Eighth grade or less
2. Some high school
3. High school graduate
4. Some college
5. Technical school or two-year (junior college) degree
6. Completed college
7. Some graduate work
8. Graduate or professional degree (M.A., Ph.D., M.D., etc.)

(37) Age (in years): _____

(38) Which of the following labels best describes your political position?
(CIRCLE ONLY ONE)

1. Liberal
2. Moderate
3. Conservative
4. Other (please describe):

---

(39) List your occupation. Please try to be as clear and specific as possible. For example, if you work as a lathe operator in a factory, you should enter "lathe operator" and not skilled tradesman, blue-collar worker, etc. If you are retired, indicate "retired" and list your principal former occupation.

---

(40) How many years have you lived in your current residence?

_____ years

(41) How far is your present home from the church you attend?
(CIRCLE ONE)

    1. Less than 1 mile
    2. 1-2 miles
    3. 2-3 miles
    4. 3-5 miles
    5. 5-10 miles
    6. More than 10 miles

(42) Where were you born?

_____

(43) In which of the categories listed below would you put your *total
family income* (from all sources, before taxes) for last year? (CIRCLE
ONE)

    1. Under $10,000
    2. $10,000-$19,999
    3. $20,000-$34,999
    4. $35,000-$49,999
    5. $50,000-$64,999
    6. $65,000-$79,999
    7. $80,000-$100,000
    8. $100,000 and over

(44) We are interested in your denominational background. In column A, CIRCLE THE NUMBER FOR THE PRESENT DENOMINATIONAL BACKGROUND. In Column B, CIRCLE THE NUMBER FOR THE DENOMINATION IN WHICH YOU WERE RAISED. In Column C, CIRCLE THE NUMBER(S), IF ANY, FOR ANY OTHER DE-NOMINATION TO WHICH YOU HAVE BELONGED.

	A Present	B Raised	C Other
AME Zion	01	01	01
United Methodist	02	02	02
Baptist	03	03	03
Roman Catholic	04	04	04
UCC/Congregational	05	05	05
Lutheran	06	06	06
Pentecostal	07	07	07
Presbyterian	08	08	08
AME	09	09	09
CME	10	10	10
None	11	11	11
Other	12	12	12

You have reached the end of the questionnaire. Thank you for your time and thoughtful consideration of the questions. You have made a valuable contribution to this study.

Introduction

1. A good introduction to these methodologies is an article by Mark Searle of Notre Dame University: "New tasks, new methods: the emergence of pastoral liturgical studies," *Worship* 57 (Jl 1983), 291-308. In this article he recommends the formation of a new area of liturgical studies: *pastoral liturgical studies,* whose object of study is "the living, offering, praying Church."

2. We are using this term to mean "artistic" or "possessed of beauty." An aesthetic object is one that displays these values to a greater or lesser extent. A baptismal font has a use in worship, but it is also an aesthetic object, because it may be decorated with symbols arranged in an artistic way.

Chapter 1

1. Anne Swidler, "Culture in action: symbols and strategies," *American Sociological Review* 51 (April 1986): 273ff.

2. Salim Kemal, "Style and Community," *The Question of Style in Philosophy and the Arts,* Caroline Van Eck, James McCallister, and Renee van de Vall, eds. (Cambridge, Mass.: Cambridge University Press, 1995), 125.

3. Nelson Goodman, *Languages of Art* (Indianapolis: Hackett Publishing Co., 1976), 241. Goodman suggests that symbols or "works" (specifically artistic symbols or works of art in these passages) not only "reorganize" our world, but are themselves "reorganized" by the way our world itself impinges upon them: "[A] symbol may select from and organize its universe and be itself in turn informed or transformed. . . . [A]esthetic experience is dynamic rather than static. It involves making delicate

discriminations and discerning subtle relationships, identifying symbol systems and characters within these systems and what these characters denote and exemplify, interpreting works and reorganizing the world in terms of works and works in terms of the world."

4. Words by William J. and Gloria Gaither & Charles Milhuff. Music by William J. Gaither. Copyright © 1970 William J. Gaither, Inc. ASCAP. All rights controlled by Gaither Copyright Management. Used by permission. See *Hymns for the Family of God* (Nashville: Paragon Associates, 1976), 313.

5. Arthur C. Danto, *The Transformation of the Commonplace* (Cambridge, Mass.: Harvard University Press, 1981), 205. "The style of a man is, to use the beautiful thought of Schopenhauer, 'the physiognomy of the soul.'"

Chapter 2

1. This quotation, and the one that follows, are taken from a handwritten account found in a notebook in the church records, titled "Historical Record."

2. Taken from "Records of the Proceedings of the quarterly conference of the ME Church at Pearsons Mills, Newbury, Mass. as revised May 1st 1858 by order of the Official Board. O. L. Butler, Preacher."

3. The practice of card-giving is discussed by Leigh Schmidt in "Practices of Exchange: From Market Culture to Gift Economy in the Interpretation of American Religion," in David D. Hall, *Lived Religion in America* (Princeton: Princeton University Press, 1997).

4. We are indebted to a brief but suggestive article by Phillippe Eberhard for this concept of mediality. See "The Mediality of Our Condition," *Journal of the American Academy of Religion* 67 (June 1999): 411-434.

5. Frank Burch Brown, *Religious Aesthetics: A Theological Study of Making and Meaning* (Princeton: Princeton University Press, 1989), 152-156.

Chapter 3

1. "Brief History of Methodism in Needham," given by Horace A. Carter at the Rally Day and semicentennial observance, Oct. 3, 1917, and published in the local newspaper.

2. "The Early Years of Methodism in Needham" (Needham, Mass: Carter Memorial United Methodist Church, 1992), 3f.

3. "Records of Quarterly and Board Meetings of the ME Church, Needham and Newton Lower Falls," Sept. 8, 1867, 3.

4. "Some Reminiscences of the Village of Highlandville," given by Sarah Elizabeth Wales at the October meeting of the Needham Historical Society, c.1911.

5. Wales, "Some Reminiscences."

6. In this chapter, I analyze the Maundy Thursday service, paying particular attention to its Tenebrae rite. I attended this service on two occasions, April 4, 1993, and March 31, 1994. Here I focus on the 1993 service and draw on the 1994 service to support key details and insights.

7. Kenneth Stevenson, *Jerusalem Revisited: the Liturgical Meaning of Holy Week* (Washington: Pastoral Press, 1984), 9.

8. Stevenson, *Jerusalem Revisited.*, 10-11.

9. These observations are based on a 3/18/96 letter of the author to Linda Clark, reflecting on the 3/16/96 meeting with the staff of Carter Church. They also draw upon a conversation with Jeanette Davies at an April 1999 project conference.

10. Anton Baumstark, *Comparative Liturgy*, revised by Bernard Botte, English edition by F. L. Cross (London: A. R. Mowbray, 1958), 27. See explanation, pp. 27-30.

11. See Bernard Botte introduction in Baumstark, *Comparative Liturgy*, viii- ix, quoted in Paul F. Bradshaw, *The Search for the Origins of Christian Worship: Sources and Methods for the Study of Early Liturgy* (New York: Oxford University Press, 1992), 61-62.

12. See a 1950s Carter Church handbook for ushers: "With your friendliness, display dignity. Remember, in no way does our sanctuary resemble the scene of a twenty-fifth anniversary class reunion. . . . Carry out your duties with self-assurance. This is not demonstrated by slouching against walls or leaning on chairs. Stand erect. Walk erect. Your position is an honor to you—respect it as you would have others respect it."

13. W. Reginald Ward and Richard Heitzenrater, eds., *John Wesley's Journal*, May 24, 1738, *The Works of John Wesley*, vol. 18, Journals and Diaries I (1735-38) (Nashville: Abingdon, 1988), 249-50.

14. Readers may not be familiar with the titles given to the various *tunes* that they sing, even well-beloved ones. For instance, they may assume that the tune called *Azmon* is "the tune" for "O For a Thousand Tongues to Sing" when that text could, in fact, be sung to *Amazing Grace* (*New Britain*), *St. Peter*, *Marsh Chapel*, or any number of other tunes composed in common meter (CM). To view the various tunes mentioned in this essay, and to see them paired with hymn texts, see *The United*

Methodist Hymnal (1989), "Metrical Index," 926-931, and "Index of Tune Names," 931-934.

15. See *The United Methodist Hymnal* (1989), 268.

16. As Lester Ruth notes in his excellent study on worship in early American Methodism, the individual experience of grace was sought in the context of fellowship. See *A Little Heaven Below: Worship at Early Methodist Quarterly Meetings* (Nashville: Abingdon, 2000), 159.

17. In mentioning the depiction of "tradition," he is, I presume, referring to Leonardo Da Vinci's painting *The Last Supper*.

18. The KJV translation of John 13:23 says the beloved disciple was "leaning on Jesus' bosom," while the NRSV translates it "the one whom Jesus loved . . . was reclining next to him." In saying that John leaned on Jesus' breast, Thompson was following the tradition established in the KJV. Indeed, the KJV gives the more literal translation of *kolpo*. In John's usage, however, the word does not necessarily refer to a spatial relationship. As Gail R. O'Day has written, this word appears in John's prologue; it is the same word used to describe the relationship of "the only Son who is close to the Father's heart," literally "in the bosom of *[kolpon]* the Father" (John 1:18). Thus, John used *kolpos* to describe a spiritual relationship, not necessarily a spatial one. See *The New Interpreter's Bible,* vol. IX, Luke-John (Nashville: Abingdon, 1995), 729.

19. Why does their piety lend itself to such a dramatic reenactment of the biblical narrative? The reasons are complex, and not entirely discernible. Of course, a community's relationship to the Scriptures is a deeply vital aspect of its piety. For all Christian communities, biblical narratives provide important paradigms for spiritual experience, yet that statement invites a further question: What does it mean, liturgically and stylistically, to be faithful to the Scriptures? For instance, the hymns of Charles Wesley, which both express and shape the piety of so many Methodist congregations, are filled with biblical allusions. In some cases, as with certain expressions of the feminist critique, one argues *against* certain aspects of the narrative; but even then, the biblical narrative is the inescapable conversation partner.

Does faithfulness to the biblical narrative require one to reenact certain aspects of that narrative, or does it allow, even *demand*, artistic and prophetic *license*? Is the story of salvation essentially finished with the completion of the biblical canon, or does the story continue to unfold, while remaining deeply rooted, inescapably so, in that canonical narrative? These are, of course, theological/liturgical questions of long duration. At its best, the church lives in creative tension between those two poles. I assume that those who gravitate toward a dramatic piety are opting for the more conservative approach to the biblical narrative, *at least during that particular moment.* When one sees such an attempt to reenact the narrative, aesthetically well-executed or not, one should ask, "What is the value that the congregation is trying to conserve?"

20. A list of Scripture texts was not printed in the bulletin, nor was a list of the Tenebrae hymns. I was able to acquire a list of the hymns, but Pastor Thompson did not give me a list of the Scriptures read. He said that such a list was not available. From what I heard and recorded in my field notes, however, I am presuming that most of the readings were from these chapters of John's Gospel. Some were, however, drawn from Matthew, Mark, and Luke.

21. Henry F. Lyte, 1847. See Carlton R. Young, ed., *The United Methodist Hymnal* (Nashville: United Methodist Publishing House, 1989), 700.

22. See Carlton R. Young, *Companion to the United Methodist Hymnal*, (Nashville: Abingdon, 1993), 685.

23. Young, *Companion to the United Methodist Hymnal*, 691.

24. Young, *Companion to the United Methodist Hymnal*, 521.

25. Sarah F. Adams, "Nearer, My God, to Thee," in *The United Methodist Hymnal*, 528.

26. Adams, "Nearer, My God."

27. See discussion by Young, *Companion to the United Methodist Hymnal*, 493. Young considers it unlikely that a *British* band on the deck of a sinking ship would have played "Nearer, My God, to Thee" *using the American tune.*

28. Charles Wesley (1742), "O Love Divine, What Hast Thou Done," *The United Methodist Hymnal*, 287.

29. Wesley, "O Love Divine."

30. Young, *Companion to the United Methodist Hymnal*, 521.

31. See *United Methodist Hymnal*, 159.

32. *United Methodist Hymnal*, 296.

33. *The Book of Common Prayer* (New York: Church Hymnal Corporation, 1979), 282. Following the devotions at the cross, the rubric says, "The hymn 'Sing, My Tongue, the Glorious Battle,' or some other hymn extolling the glory of the cross, is then sung.

34. See *The United Methodist Hymnal*, 296, vss. 1,5.

35. Frank Burch Brown, *Religious Aesthetics: A Theological Study*

of Making and Meaning (Princeton: Princeton University Press, 1989), 98-99.

36. *The United Methodist Hymnal*, respectively, hymn numbers 424, 504, 358, 687, and 282.

37. John Wesley, "The Almost Christian" (1741), Albert C. Outler, ed., *The Works of John Wesley*, vol. 1. (Nashville: Abingdon, 1984), 131-141.

38. Wesley, "The Almost Christian," 132.

39. Wesley, "The Almost Christian," 137-138.

40. Don E. Saliers, *The Soul in Paraphrase: Prayer and the Religious Affections*, 2nd edition (Akron, Ohio: OSL Publications, 1980, 1991), 9, 77.

41. Saliers, *The Soul in Paraphrase*, 8-9, 48.

42. Charles Grandison Finney, *Revival Lectures,* 1835 (Old Tappan, N.J.: Fleming H. Revell, n.d.), 4.

Chapter 4

1. Adelaide M. Cromwell, *The Other Brahmins* (Fayetteville: University of Arkansas Press, 1994), 79f.

2. "Historical Sketch of A.M.E. Zion Church, Boston, Mass, U. S. A.," Jacob Wesley Powell, *A Bird's Eye View of the General Conference of the AME Zion Church,* (Malden, 1918), 21.

3. *Courage and Conscience*: *Black and White Abolitionists in Boston*, 171. (no author, city or publisher given).

4. *Courage and Conscience,* 175.

5. *Courage and Conscience*, 178.

6. James and Lois E. Horton, *Black Bostonians: Family Life and Community Struggles in the Antebellum North* (New York: Holmes and Meier, 1979), 3.

7. Robert C. Hayden, *Faith, Culture and Leadership: A History of the Black Church in Boston* (Boston: Boston Branch, NAACP and Robert Hayden, 1983), 24.

8. Elizabeth Pleck, *Black Migration and Poverty, Boston 1865-1900* (New York: Academic Press, 1979), 51.

9. Pleck, *Black Migration and Poverty*, 61.

10. Pleck, *Black Migration and Poverty,* 77.

11. Eileen Southern, "Musical Practices in Black Churches of Philadelphia and New York, ca. 1800–1844," *Journal of the American Musicological Association* 30 (summer 1977), 309f.

Chapter 5

1. Henry N. Wieman, *The Source of Human Good* (Chicago: University of Chicago Press, 1946), 56.

2. Wieman, *Source of Human Good,* 24.

3. Dan Herr, "An Agenda for Vatican III," *Notre Dame Magazine* (Oct. 1982): 25; quoted in Mark Searle, "The Emergence of Pastoral Liturgical Studies," *Worship* 57 (July 1983): 292.

4. Wieman, *Source of Human Good*, 57.

Appendix C

1. A "cradle" Methodist is one who was born a Methodist. A "switcher" became one sometime later in life.